My Dear Mrs. Jacobs.

Will you let this little volume sometimes remind you, that your loving care of our sister and the tender sympathy with which you so often received those, who loved her and suffered with her, will ever be gratefully and lovingly remembered by

Your sincerely attached friend

Carrie M. Smith

Dec. 25th. 1864

Lyra Germanica:

HYMNS FOR THE SUNDAYS AND CHIEF FESTIVALS OF THE CHRISTIAN YEAR.

Lyra Germanica.

HYMNS FOR THE SUNDAYS AND CHIEF FESTIVALS OF THE CHRISTIAN YEAR.

TRANSLATED FROM THE GERMAN BY

CATHERINE WINKWORTH.

A NEW EDITION.

BOSTON:
E. P. DUTTON AND COMPANY,
106 WASHINGTON STREET.
1862.

TO HIS EXCELLENCY

THE CHEVALIER BUNSEN,

ETC. ETC. ETC.

THESE HYMNS ARE, BY HIS KIND PERMISSION,

RESPECTFULLY AND GRATEFULLY

DEDICATED BY

THE TRANSLATOR.

PREFACE.

THE following hymns are ſelected from the Chevalier Bunſen's "Verſuch eines allgemeinen Geſang und Gebetbuchs," publiſhed in 1833. From the large number there given, about nine hundred, little more than one hundred have been choſen. This ſelection contains many of thoſe beſt known and loved in Germany, but in a work of this ſize it is impoſſible to include all that have become claſſical in that home of Chriſtian poetry. In reading them it muſt be remembered that they are hymns, not ſacred poems, though from their length and the intricacy of their metres, many of them may ſeem to Engliſh readers adapted rather to purpoſes of private than of public devotion. But the ſinging of hymns forms a much larger and more important part of public worſhip in the German

Reformed Churches than in our own ſervices. It is the mode by which the whole congregation is enabled to bear its part in the worſhip of God, anſwering in this reſpect to the chanting of our own Liturgy.

Ever ſince the Reformation, the German church has been remarkable for the number and excellence of its hymns and hymn-tunes. Before that time it was not ſo. There was no place for congregational ſinging in public worſhip, and therefore the ſpiritual ſongs of the latter part of the middle ages aſſumed for the moſt part an artificial and unpopular form. Yet there were not wanting germs of a national Church poetry in the verſes rather than hymns which were ſung in German on pilgrimages and at ſome of the high feſtivals, many of which verſes were again derived from more ancient Latin hymns. Several of Luther's hymns are amplifications of verſes of this claſs, ſuch as the Pentecoſtal hymn here given, "Come, Holy Spirit, God and Lord,"* which is founded on a German verſion of the "Veni Sancte Spiritus, Reple." By adopting theſe verſes, and retaining their well-known melodies, Luther enabled his hymns

* Page 117.

to ſpread rapidly among the common people. He alſo compoſed metrical verſions of ſeveral of the Pſalms, the Te Deum, the Ten Commandments, the Lord's Prayer, the Nunc Dimittis, the Da nobis Pacem, &c. thus enriching the people, to whom he had already given the Holy Scriptures in their own language, with a treaſure of that ſacred poetry which is the precious inheritance of every Chriſtian Church.

The hymn, "In the midſt of life,"* is one of thoſe founded on a more ancient hymn, the "Media in vita" of Notker, a learned Benedictine of St. Gall, who died in 912. He is ſaid to have compoſed it while watching ſome workmen, who were building the bridge of Martinsbruck at the peril of their lives. It was ſoon ſet to muſic, and became univerſally known; indeed it was used as a battle-ſong, until the cuſtom was forbidden on account of its being ſuppoſed to exerciſe magical influences. In a German verſion it formed part of the ſervice for the burial of the dead, as early as the thirteenth century, and is ſtill preſerved in an unmetrical form in the Burial Service of our own Church.

* Page 235.

The carol, "From Heaven above to earth I come,"* is called by Luther himſelf, "a Chriſtmas child's ſong concerning the child Jeſus." He wrote it for his little boy Hans, when the latter was five years old, and it is ſtill ſung from the dome of the Kreuzkirche in Dreſden before day-break on the morning of Chriſtmas Day. It refers to the cuſtom then and long afterwards prevalent in Germany, of making at Chriſtmas-time repreſentations of the manger with the infant Jeſus. But the moſt famous of his hymns is his noble verſion of the 46th Pſalm, "God is my ſtronghold firm and ſure,"† which may be called the national hymn of his Proteſtant countrymen. Luther's hymns are wanting in harmony and correctneſs of metre to a degree which often makes them jarring to our modern ears, but they are always full of fire and ſtrength, of clear Chriſtian faith, and brave joyful truſt in God.

From this time there has been a conſtant ſucceſſion of hymn-writers in the German church. Paul Eber, an intimate friend of Melancthon, wrote for his chil-

* Page 12. † Page 173.

dren the hymn, "Lord Jeſus Chriſt, true Man and God,"* which ſoon became a favourite hymn for the dying. Hugo Grotius aſked that it might be repeated to him in his laſt moments, and expired ere its conclusion. Another hymn of the ſame claſs is, "O weep not, mourn not, o'er this bier,"† the "Jam mœſta quieſce querela" of Prudentius II. tranſlated by Nicholas Hermann, the pious old precentor of Joachimſthal, a hymn long ſung at every funeral.

The terrible times of the Thirty Years' War were rich in ſacred poetry. Riſt, a clergyman in North Germany, who ſuffered much in his youth from mental conflicts, and in after years from plunder, peſtilence, and all the horrors of war, uſed to ſay, "the dear croſs hath preſſed many ſongs out of me," and this ſeems to have been equally true of many of his contemporaries. It certainly was true of Johann Heermann, the author of ſome of the moſt touching hymns for Paſſion Week, who wrote his ſweet ſongs under great phyſical ſuffering from ill health, and amidſt the perils of war, during which he more than once eſcaped murder as by a miracle. So too the

* Page 239. † Page 249.

hymns of Simon Dach,* professor of poetry in the University of Konigsberg, speak of the sufferings of the Christian, and his longing to escape from the strife of earth to the peace of heaven.

But the Christians of those days had often not only to suffer, but to fight for their faith, and in the hymns of Altenburg and von Lowenstern we have two that may be called battle-songs of the church. The former published his hymn, "Fear not, O little flock, the foe,"† in 1631, with this title: "A heart-cheering song of comfort on the watchword of the Evangelical Army in the battle of Leipsic, September 7th, 1631, God with us." It was called Gustavus Adolphus' battle-song, because the pious hero often sang it with his army; and he sang it for the last time immediately before the battle of Lutzen. The latter, von Lowenstern, was the son of a saddler, whom the Emperor, Ferdinand III. ennobled for his public services: he was at once a statesman, poet, and musician. His hymn, "Christ, Thou the champion of the band,"‡ was a favourite of Niebuhr.

* Pages 129 and 252. † Page 17.
‡ Page 105.

Another favourite hymn of Niebuhr was the hymn to Eternity,* the greater part of which is of very ancient but uncertain date. It received its present form about the middle of the 17th century.

Many of the hymns of Paul Gerhardt belong to this period, though he lived until 1676, long after the conclusion of peace. He is without doubt the greatest of the German hymn-writers, possessing loftier poetical genius, and a richer variety of thought and feeling than any other. His beautiful hymn, "Commit thou all thy ways," is already well known to us through Wesley's translation, and many others of his are not inferior to it. He was a zealous preacher for several years at the Nicolai-Kirche in Berlin; whence he retired because he had not sufficient freedom in preaching the truth, and became Archdeacon of Lubben. With him culminated the elder school of German sacred poetry, a school distinguished by its depth and simplicity. Most of its hymns are either written for the high festivals and services of the Church, or are expressive of a simple Christian faith, ready to dare or suffer all things for God's sake. To this

* Page 24.

ſchool we muſt refer, from their ſpirit, two hymns written a little later; the firſt is, "Jeſus my Redeemer lives,"* one of the moſt favourite Eaſter hymns, written by the pious Electreſs of Brandenburg, who founded the Orphan Houſe at Oranienburg. The other, "Leave God to order all thy ways,"† was written by George Neumarck, Secretary of the Archives at Weimar. It ſpread rapidly among the common people, at firſt without the author's name. A baker's boy in New Brandenburg uſed to ſing it over his work, and ſoon the whole town and neighbourhood flocked to him to learn this beautiful new ſong.

In the latter half of the ſeventeenth century a new ſchool was founded by Johann Franck, and Johann Scheffler, commonly called Angelus. The former was burgomaſter of Guben in Luſatia; the latter phyſician to Ferdinand III.; but in 1663 he became a Roman Catholic, and afterwards a prieſt. The pervading idea of this ſchool is the longing of the ſoul for that intimate union with the Redeemer of the world, which begins with the birth of Chriſt in the heart, and is perfected after death. This longing

* Page 93. † Page 152.

breathes through the hymns of Franck given in this collection; one of them, "Redeemer of the nations, come,"* is a translation of the "Veni, Redemptor gentium" of St. Ambrose. Angelus dwells rather on the means of attaining this union by the sacrifice of the Self to God through the great High-priest of mankind, an idea expressed in his hymns with peculiar tenderness and sweetness. We find much of his spirit and sweetness lingering in modern times about the few hymns of the gifted Novalis.

The greatest poet of this school is however Gerhardt Tersteegen, who lived during the early part of the eighteenth century as a ribbon manufacturer at Muhlheim. His hymns have great beauty, and bespeak a tranquil and childlike soul filled and blessed with the contemplation of God. The well-known hymn of Wesley's, "Lo God is here! let us adore," belongs to him, and in its original shape is one of the most beautiful he ever wrote, but is frequently met with only in a disfigured and mutilated form. To this school belong a large number of the hymns in this collection, among which those of Deszler,† an

* Page 186. † Pages 59, 147.

excellent philologiſt of Nuremberg, and of Anton Ulrich,* the pious and learned Duke of Brunſwick, are particularly good. Thoſe of Schmolck, the paſtor of Schweidnitz, who exerciſed great influence over the hymn-writing of his day, have more ſimplicity than moſt of the reſt, but are characteriſed by a curious mixture of real poetry and deep feeling with occaſional vulgarities of expreſſion. The defects of this ſchool, which ſhowed themſelves ſtrongly in the courſe of the eighteenth century, were a tendency that the feeling ſhould degenerate into ſentimentality, and the devout dwelling of the heart on Chriſt's great ſacrifice into compaſſion and gratitude for His phyſical ſufferings,—defects which greatly disfigure many of the Moravian hymns. In ſome of the hymns here tranſlated the expreſſion "Chriſti Wundenhohle" occurs, which has been rendered by the blood or croſs of Chriſt, as being phraſes at once more ſcriptural and more conſonant to our feelings. There were not wanting however, even at this period, many hymns fit for good ſoldiers of Jeſus Chriſt, ſuch as "Who ſeeks in weakneſs his excuſe,"† and others of the ſame kind.

---

* Pages 145, 159, 220. † Page 149.

Germany is rich in Morning and Evening Hymns, and Hymns for the Dying, of which a few are given in theſe tranſlations. Among theſe is the morning hymn of Baron von Canitz: I was not aware until after tranſlating it that it had been already publiſhed at the cloſe of one volume of Dr. Arnold's ſermons.

The hymn "How bleſt to all Thy followers, Lord, the road,"* was the favourite hymn of Schelling.

In tranſlating theſe hymns the original form has been retained with the exception, that ſingle rhymes are almoſt invariably ſubſtituted for the double rhymes which the ſtructure of the language renders ſo common in German poetry, but which become cloying to an Engliſh ear when often repeated; and that Engliſh double common or ſhort metre is uſed inſtead of what may be called the German common metre, the ſame that we call Gay's ſtanza, which is ſcarcely ſolemn enough for ſacred purpoſes. In a few inſtances ſlight alterations have been made in the metre, when, as is the caſe with ſome excellent hymns in our own language, it is hardly grave and dignified enough for the poetry. Theſe alterations are but

* Page 175.

ſlight, and ſeemed juſtifiable, ſince theſe hymns have been tranſlated, not ſo much as ſpecimens of German hymn-writing, as in the hope that theſe utterances of Chriſtian piety which have comforted and ſtrengthened the hearts of many true Chriſtians in their native country, may ſpeak to the hearts of ſome among us, to help and cheer thoſe who muſt ſtrive and ſuffer, and to make us feel afreſh what a deep and true Communion of Saints exiſts among all the children of God in different churches and lands.

Alderley Edge,
July 16th, 1855.

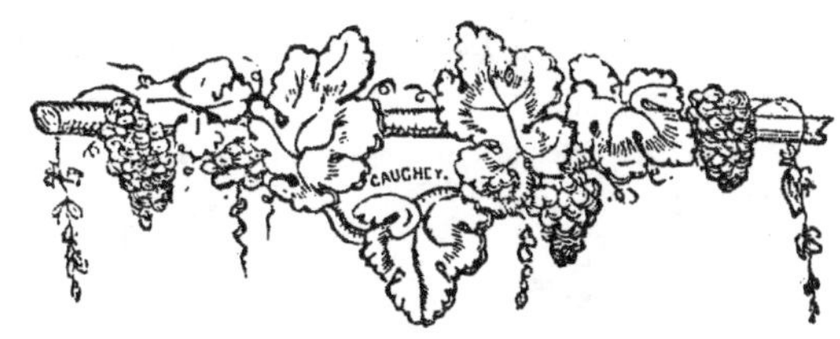

CONTENTS.

Lyra Germanica.

FIRST SUNDAY IN ADVENT.

The night is far ſpent, the day is at hand; let us therefore caſt off the works of darkneſs, and put on the armour of light.—FROM THE EPISTLE.

O WATCHMAN, will the night of ſin
Be never paſt?
O watchman, doth the day begin
To dawn upon thy ſtraining ſight at laſt?
Will it diſpel
Ere long the miſts of ſenſe wherein I dwell?

Now all the earth is bright and glad
With the freſh morn;
But all my heart is cold and dark and ſad;
Sun of the ſoul, let me behold Thy dawn!
Come Jeſus, Lord!
Oh quickly come, according to Thy word!

Do we not live in thoſe bleſt days
So long foretold,
When Thou ſhouldſt come to bring us light and grace?
And yet I ſit in darkneſs as of old,
Pining to ſee
Thy glory; but Thou ſtill art far from me.

Long ſince Thou cam'ſt to be the light
Of all men here;
And yet in me is nought but blackeſt night.
Wilt Thou not then to me, Thine own, appear?
Shine forth and bleſs
My ſoul with viſion of Thy righteouſneſs!

If thus in darkneſs ever left,
Can I fulfil
The works of light, while of all light bereft?
How ſhall I learn in love and meekneſs ſtill
To follow Thee,
And all the ſinful works of darkneſs flee?

The light of reaſon cannot give
Life to my ſoul;
Jeſus alone can make me truly live,
One glance of His can make my ſpirit whole.
Ariſe, and ſhine
On this poor longing, waiting heart of mine!

Single and clear, not weak or blind,
The eye muſt be,

To which Thy glory ſhall an entrance find;
For if Thy choſen ones would gaze on Thee,
No earthly ſcreen
Between their ſouls and Thee muſt intervene.

Jeſus, do Thou mine eyes unſeal,
And let them grow
Quick to diſcern whate'er Thou doſt reveal,
So ſhall I be deliver'd from that woe,
Blindly to ſtray
Through hopeleſs night, while all around is day.

Richter. 1704.

SECOND SUNDAY IN ADVENT.

Behold the fig-tree and all the trees; when they now ſhoot forth, ye ſee and know of your own ſelves that ſummer is now nigh at hand. So likewiſe ye, when ye ſee that theſe things come to paſs, know ye that the kingdom of God is nigh at hand.—FROM THE GOSPEL.

AWAKE, thou careleſs world, awake!
The final day ſhall ſurely come;
What Heaven hath fixed Time cannot ſhake,
It cannot ſweep away thy doom.
Know, what the Lord Himſelf hath ſpoken
Shall come at laſt and not delay,
Though heaven and earth ſhall paſs away,
His ſteadfaſt word can ne'er be broken.

Awake! He comes to judgment, wake!
Sinners behold His countenance
In beauty terrible, and quake
Condemn'd beneath His piercing glance.
Lo He to whom all power is given,
Who ſits at God's right hand on high,
In fire and thunder draweth nigh
To judge all nations under Heaven.

Awake, thou carelefs world, awake!
　Who knows how foon our God fhall please
That fuddenly that day fhould break;
　We fathom not fuch depths as thefe.
O guard thee well from luft and greed,
　For as the bird is in the fnare,
　Or ever of its foe aware,
So comes that day with filent fpeed.

The Lord in love delayeth long
　The final day, and grants us fpace
To turn away from fin and wrong,
　And mourning feek His help and grace.
He holdeth back that beft of days,
　Until the righteous fhall approve
　Their faith and hope, their conftant love;
So gentle us-ward are His ways!

But ye, O faithful fouls, fhall fee
　That morning rife in love and joy;
Your Saviour comes to fet you free,
　Your Judge fhall all your bonds deftroy;
He, the true Jofhua, then fhall bring
　His people with a mighty hand,
　Into their promifed father-land,
Where fongs of victory they fhall fing.

Rejoice! the fig-tree fhows her green,
　The fpringing year is in its prime,
The little flowers afrefh are feen,
　We gather ftrength in this great time.

The glorious ſummer draweth near,
When all this body's earthly load,
In light that morning ſheds abroad,
Shall wax as ſunshine pure and clear.

Ariſe, and let us day and night
Pray in the Spirit ceaſeleſsly,
That we may heed our Lord aright,
And ever in His preſence be.
Ariſe, and let us haſte to meet
The Bridegroom ſtanding at the door,
That with the angels evermore
We too may worſhip at His feet.

Rist. 1651.

THIRD SUNDAY IN ADVENT.

And it ſhall be ſaid in that day; Lo! this is our God, we have waited for Him, and He will ſave us; this is the Lord, we have waited for Him, and we will rejoice in His ſalvation.—From the Lesson.

HOW ſhall I meet Thee? How my heart
Receive her Lord aright?
Deſire of all the earth Thou art!
My hope, my ſole delight!
Kindle the lamp, Thou Lord, alone,
Half dying in my breaſt,
And make thy gracious pleaſure known
How I may greet Thee beſt.

Her budding boughs and faireſt palms
Thy Zion ſtrews around;
And ſongs of praiſe and ſweeteſt pſalms
From my glad heart ſhall ſound.
My deſert ſoul breaks forth in flowers,
Rejoicing in Thy fame;
And puts forth all her ſleeping powers
To honour Jeſus' name.

In heavy bonds I languiſh'd long,
Thou com'ſt to ſet me free;
The ſcorn of every mocking tongue—
Thou com'ſt to honour me.

A heavenly crown Thou doſt beſtow,
And gifts of priceleſs worth,
That vaniſh not as here below
The riches of the earth.

Nought, nought, dear Lord! had power to move
Thee from Thy rightful place,
Save that almighty wondrous Love
Wherewith Thou doſt embrace
This weary world and all her woe,
Her load of grief and ill
And ſorrow, more than man can know;
Thy love is deeper ſtill.

Oh write this promiſe in your heart,
Ye ſad at heart, with whom
Sorrows fall thick, and joys depart,
And darker grows your gloom.
Deſpair not, for your help is near,
He ſtandeth at the door
Who beſt can comfort you and cheer,
He comes, nor ſtayeth more.

Vex not your ſouls with care, nor grieve
And labour longer thus,
As though your arm could ought achieve,
And bring Him down to us!
He comes, He comes with ready will,
By pity moved alone,
All pain to ſoothe, all tears to ſtill,
To Him they all are known.

Ye ſhall not ſhrink nor turn aſide,
  Fearing to ſee His face
So deep your ſins, for He will hide
  The darkeſt with His grace.
He comes, He comes, to ſave from ſin,
  All ſinners to releaſe,
For all the ſons of God to win
  The heritage of peace.

Why aſk ye what the wicked ſaith,
  Why heed his craft and ſpite?
The Lord deſtroys him with a breath,
  He ſtands not in His ſight.
Chriſt comes, He comes, as King to reign!
  Then gather ye His foes,
From earth's far corners; yet in vain
  Would ye His rule oppoſe.

He comes to judge the earth, and ye
  Who mock'd Him, feel His wrath;
But they who loved and ſought Him ſee
  His light o'er all their path.
O Sun of Righteouſneſs! ariſe,
  And guide us on our way,
To yon fair manſion in the ſkies
  Of joyous, cloudleſs day.

PAUL GERHARDT. 1653

FOURTH SUNDAY IN ADVENT

Rejoice in the Lord alway, and again I ſay unto you, Rejoice . . . The Lord is at hand.—FROM THE EPISTLE.

LIFT up your heads, ye mighty gates,
Behold the King of glory waits,
The King of kings is drawing near,
The Saviour of the world is here;
Life and ſalvation doth He bring,
Wherefore rejoice, and gladly ſing
Praiſe, O my God, to Thee!
Creator, wiſe is Thy decree!

The Lord is juſt, a helper tried,
Mercy is ever at His ſide,
His kingly crown is holineſs,
His ſceptre, pity in diſtreſs,
The end of all our woe He brings;
Wherefore the earth is glad and ſings
Praiſe, O my God, to Thee!
O Saviour, great Thy deeds ſhall be!

Oh, bleſt the land, the city bleſt,
Where Chriſt the ruler is confeſt!
O happy hearts and happy homes
To whom this King in triumph comes!

The cloudless Sun of joy He is,
Who bringeth pure delight and bliss;
    Praise, O my God, to Thee!
    Comforter, for Thy comfort free!

Fling wide the portals of your heart,
Make it a temple set apart
From earthly use for Heaven's employ,
Adorn'd with prayer, and love, and joy;
So shall your Sovereign enter in,
And new and nobler life begin.
    Praise, O my God, be Thine,
    For word, and deed, and grace divine.

Redeemer, come! I open wide
My heart to Thee, here, Lord, abide!
Let me Thy inner presence feel,
Thy grace and love in me reveal,
Thy Holy Spirit guide us on
Until our glorious goal be won!
    Eternal praise and fame,
    Be offer'd, Saviour, to Thy Name!

WEISZEL. 1635.

CHRISTMAS EVE.

A Carol.

Behold I bring you good tidings of great joy that ſhall be to all people.—Luke ii. 10.

FROM heaven above to earth I come
To bear good news to every home;
Glad tidings of great joy I bring,
Whereof I now will ſay and ſing:

To you, this night, is born a child
Of Mary, choſen mother mild;
This little child, of lowly birth,
Shall be the joy of all your earth.

'Tis Chriſt our God, who far on high
Hath heard your ſad and bitter cry;
Himſelf will your Salvation be,
Himſelf from ſin will make you free.

He brings thoſe bleſſings, long ago
Prepared by God for all below;
Henceforth, His kingdom open ſtands
To you, as to the angel bands.

Theſe are the tokens ye ſhall mark,
The ſwaddling clothes and manger dark

There ſhall ye find the young child laid,
By whom the heavens and earth were made.

Now let us all with gladſome cheer,
Follow the ſhepherds, and draw near,
To ſee this wondrous gift of God
Who hath His only Son beſtowed.

Give heed, my heart, lift up thine eyes!
Who is it in yon manger lies?
Who is this child ſo young and fair?
The bleſſed Chriſt-child lieth there.

Welcome to earth, Thou noble gueſt,
Through whom e'en wicked men are bleſt!
Thou com'ſt to ſhare our miſery,
What can we render, Lord, to Thee!

Ah, Lord, who haſt created all,
How haſt Thou made Thee weak and ſmall,
That Thou muſt chooſe Thy infant bed
Where aſs and ox but lately fed!

Were earth a thouſand times as fair
Beſet with gold and jewels rare,
She yet were far too poor to be,
A narrow cradle, Lord, for Thee.

For velvets ſoft and ſilken ſtuff
Thou haſt but hay, and ſtraw ſo rough,
Whereon Thou king, ſo rich and great,
As 'twere Thy heaven, art throned in ſtate.

Thus hath it pleaſed Thee to make plain
The truth to us poor fools and vain,
That this world's honour, wealth and might
Are nought and worthleſs in Thy ſight.

Ah deareſt Jeſus, Holy Child,
Make Thee a bed, ſoft, undefiled,
Within my heart, that it may be
A quiet chamber kept for Thee.

My heart for very joy doth leap,
My lips no more can ſilence keep;
I too muſt ſing with joyful tongue
That ſweeteſt ancient cradle-ſong—

Glory to God in higheſt Heaven,
Who unto man His Son hath given!
While angels ſing with pious mirth
A glad New Year to all the earth.

LUTHER.

Written for his little ſon Hans. 1540.

CHRISTMAS DAY.

And the Word was made flesh, and dwelt among us.
FROM THE GOSPEL.

O THOU essential Word,
Who from eternity
Dwelt with the Father and wast God,
Who art ordain'd to be
The Saviour of our race;
Welcome indeed Thou art,
Blessed Redeemer, Fount of Grace,
To this my longing heart!

Come, self-existent Word,
Within my spirit speak,
In that blest soul where Thou art heard
Peace dwells without a break.
Light of the world, abide
Through faith within my heart,
Leave me to seek no other guide,
Nor e'er from Thee depart.

Why didst thou leave Thy throne,
O Jesus, what could bring
Thee to a world where e'en Thine own
Knew not their rightful King?
Thy love beyond all thought,
Stronger than Death or Hell,
And my deep woe, this wonder wrought
That Thou on earth dost dwell.

Wherefore I fain would give
My heart and ſoul, dear Lord,
To ſerve Thee only while I live
And ſpread Thy fame abroad.
O Jeſus, take away
This ſtony heart of mine!
Give me another heart, I pray,
That ſhall be wholly Thine.

Let nought be left within
But cometh of Thy hand;
Root quickly out the weeds of ſin,
My cunning foe withſtand.
From Thee comes nothing ill,
'Tis he doth ſet the tares;
Make plain my path before me ſtill,
Save me from all his ſnares.

Thou art the Life, O Lord!
Sole Light of Life Thou art!
Let not Thy glorious rays be pour'd
In vain on my dark heart.
Star of the Eaſt, ariſe!
Drive all my clouds away,
Guide me till earth's dim twilight dies
Into the perfect day!

LAURENTI. 1700.

ST. STEPHEN'S DAY.

I have ſeen, I have ſeen the afflictions of my people.
FROM THE LESSON.

FEAR not, O little flock, the foe
Who madly ſeeks your overthrow,
Dread not his rage and power.
What though your courage ſometimes faints,
His ſeeming triumph o'er God's ſaints
Laſts but a little hour.

Be of good cheer; your cauſe belongs
To Him who can avenge your wrongs,
Leave it to Him our Lord.
Though hidden yet from all our eyes,
He ſees the Gideon who ſhall riſe
To ſave us, and His word.

As true as God's own word is true,
Not earth or hell with all their crew
Againſt us ſhall prevail.
A jeſt and byword are they grown;
God is with us, we are His own,
Our victory cannot fail.

Amen, Lord Jeſus, grant our prayer!
Great Captain, now Thine arm make bare;
Fight for us once again!
So ſhall The ſaints and martyrs raiſe
A mighty chorus to Thy praiſe,
World without end. Amen.

ALTENBURG.

Guſtavus Adolphus' Battle-ſong. 1631.

ST. JOHN THE EVANGELIST.

If I will that he tarry till I come, what is that to thee? Follow thou me.—FROM THE GOSPEL.

IF Thou, True Life, wilt in me live,
Consume whate'er is not of Thee;
One look of Thine more joy can give
Than all the world can offer me.
O Jesus, be Thou mine for ever,
Nought from Thy Love my heart can sever,
That Thou hast promised in Thy Word;
Oh deep the joy whereof I drink,
Whene'er my soul in Thee can sink,
And own her Bridegroom and her Lord.

O Heart, that glow'd with love and died,
Kindle my soul with fire divine;
Lord, in the heart Thou'st won, abide,
And all in it that is not Thine
Oh let me conquer and destroy,
Strong in Thy love, Thou Fount of Joy.
Nay, be Thou conqueror, Lord, in me;
So shall I triumph o'er despair,
O'er death itself Thy victory share,
Thus suffer, live, and die in Thee.

And let the fire within me move
  My heart to ſerve Thy members here;
Let me their need and trials prove,
  That I may know my love ſincere
And like to Thine, Lord, pure and warm;
For when my ſoul hath won that form
Is likeſt to Thy holy mind,
  Then I ſhall love both friends and foes,
  And learn to grieve o'er others' woes,
Like Thee, my Pattern, true and kind.

The light and ſtrength of faith, oh grant,
  That I may bring forth holy fruit,
A living branch, a blooming plant,
  Faſt clinging to my vine—my root.
Thou art my Saviour, whom I truſt,
My Rock,—I build not on the duſt,—
The ground of faith, eternal, ſure.
  When hours of doubt o'ercloud my mind,
  Thy ready help then let me find,
Thy ſtrength my ſickening ſpirit cure.

Nor let my hope e'er fade away,—
  Thy croſs the anchor of my heart,—
But let her riſe o'er fear, diſmay,
  Conqueror through Thee; mine All Thou art.
The world may build on what decays,
O Chriſt, my Sun of Hope, my gaze
Cares not o'er leſſer lights to range;
  To Thee, in Love, I ever cleave,
  For well I know Thou ne'er wilt leave
My ſoul, Thy love can never change.

Wouldſt Thou that I ſhould tarry here,
  I live becauſe Thou willeſt it:
Or Death ſhould ſuddenly appear,
  I ſhall not fear him, Lord, one whit,
If but Thy Life ſtill in me live;
Thy holy death my ſtrength ſhall give
When earthly life draws near its end;
  To Thee I give away my will,
  In life and death remembering ſtill
Thou ſeek'ſt my good, O trueſt Friend.

SINOLD. 1710.

INNOCENTS' DAY.

Except ye be converted, and become as little children, ye ſhall not enter into the kingdom of Heaven.
MATT. xviii. 3.

DEAR Soul, couldſt thou become a child
While yet on earth, meek, undefiled,
Then God Himſelf were ever near,
And Paradiſe around thee here.

A child cares nought for gold or treaſure,
Nor fame nor glory yield him pleaſure;
In perfect truſt, he aſketh not
If rich or poor ſhall be his lot.

Little he recks of dignity,
Nor prince nor monarch feareth he;
Strange that a child ſo weak and ſmall
Is oft the boldeſt of us all!

He hath not ſkill to utter lies,
His very ſoul is in his eyes;
Single his aim in all, and true,
And apt to praiſe what others do.

No queſtions dark his ſpirit vex,
No faithleſs doubts his ſoul perplex,
Simply from day to day he lives,
Content with what the preſent gives.

Scarce can he ſtand alone, far leſs
Would roam abroad in lonelineſs;
Faſt clinging to his mother ſtill,
She bears and leads him at her will.

He will not ſtay to pauſe and chooſe,
His Father's guidance e'er refuſe,
Thinks not of danger, fears no harm,
Wrapt in obedience' holy calm.

For ſtrange concerns he careth nought;
What others do, although were wrought
Before his eyes the worſt offence,
Stains not his tranquil innocence.

His deareſt work, his beſt delight,
Is, lying in his mother's ſight,
To gaze forever on her face,
And neſtle in her fond embrace.

O childhood's innocence! the voice
Of thy deep wiſdom is my choice!
Who hath thy lore is truly wiſe,
And precious in our Father's eyes.

Spirit of childhood! loved of God,
By Jeſus' Spirit now beſtowed;
How often have I long'd for thee;
O Jeſus, form Thyſelf in me!

And help me to become a child
While yet on earth, meek, undefiled,
That I may find God always near,
And Paradiſe around me here.

Gerhardt Tersteegen. 1731.

SUNDAY AFTER CHRISTMAS DAY.

Behold a Virgin ſhall be with child, and ſhall bring forth a Son, and they ſhall call his name Emmanuel, which being interpreted is, God with us.

FROM THE GOSPEL.

THEE, O Immanuel, we praiſe,
The Prince of Life, and Fount of Grace,
The Morning Star, the Heavenly
Flower,
The Virgin's Son, the Lord of Power!

With all Thy ſaints, Thee, Lord, we ſing,
Praiſe, honour, thanks to Thee we bring,
That Thou, O long-expected gueſt,
Haſt come at laſt to make us bleſt!

E'er ſince the world began to be,
How many a heart hath longed for Thee;
Long years our fathers hoped of old
Their eyes might yet Thy Light behold.

The prophets cried: "Ah, would He came
To break the fetters of our ſhame;
That help from Zion came to men,
Iſrael were glad, and proſper'd then!"

Now art Thou here; we know Thee now
In lowly manger lieſt Thou;
A child, yet makeſt all things great,
Poor, yet is earth Thy robe of ſtate.

All heavens are Thine, yet Thou doſt come
To ſojourn in a ſtranger's home;
Thou hangeſt on Thy mother's breaſt
Who art the joy of ſpirits bleſt.

Now fearleſs I can look on Thee,
From ſin and grief Thou ſett'ſt me free;
Thou beareſt wrath, Thou conquereſt Death,
Fear turns to joy Thy glance beneath.

Thou art my Head, my Lord Divine,
I am Thy member, wholly Thine,
And in Thy Spirit's ſtrength would ſtill
Serve Thee according to Thy will.

Thus will I ſing Thy praiſes here
With joyful ſpirit year by year;
And they ſhall ſound before Thy throne,
Where time nor number more are known.

PAUL GERHARDT. 1650.

THE CIRCUMCISION OF CHRIST.

Hymn for New Year's Day.

So teach us to number our days that we may apply our hearts unto wiſdom.—Psalm xc. 12.

ETERNITY! Eternity!
How long art thou, Eternity!
And yet to thee Time haſtes away,
Like as the warhorſe to the fray,
Or ſwift as couriers homeward go,
Or ſhip to port, or ſhaft from bow.
Ponder, O Man, Eternity!

Eternity! Eternity!
How long art thou, Eternity!
For even as on a perfect ſphere
End nor beginning can appear,
Even ſo, Eternity, in thee
Entrance nor Exit can there be.
Ponder, O Man, Eternity!

Eternity! Eternity!
How long art thou, Eternity!
A circle infinite art thou,
Thy centre an Eternal Now,
Never, we name thy outward bound,
For never end therein is found.
Ponder, O Man, Eternity!

Eternity! Eternity!
How long art thou, Eternity!
A little bird with fretting beak
Might wear to nought the loftieſt peak,
Though but each thouſand years it came,
Yet thou wert then, as now, the ſame.
Ponder, O Man, Eternity!

Eternity! Eternity!
How long art thou, Eternity!
As long as God is God, ſo long
Endure the pains of hell and wrong,
So long the joys of heaven remain;
Oh laſting joy, Oh laſting pain!
Ponder, O Man, Eternity!

Eternity! Eternity!
How long art thou, Eternity!
O Man, full oft thy thoughts ſhould dwell
Upon the pains of ſin and hell,
And on the glories of the pure,
That both beyond all time endure.
Ponder, O Man, Eternity!

Eternity! Eternity!
How long art thou, Eternity!
How terrible art thou in woe,
How fair where joys for ever glow!
God's goodneſs ſheddeth gladneſs here,
His juſtice there wakes bitter fear.
Ponder, O Man, Eternity!

Eternity! Eternity!
How long art thou, Eternity!
They who lived poor and naked reſt
With God for ever rich and bleſt,
And love and praiſe the higheſt good,
In perfect bliſs and gladſome mood.
Ponder, O Man, Eternity!

Eternity! Eternity!
How long art thou, Eternity!
A moment laſts all joy below,
Whereby man ſinks to endleſs woe,
A moment laſts all earthly pain,
Whereby an endleſs joy we gain.
Ponder, O Man, Eternity!

Eternity! Eternity!
How long art thou, Eternity!
Who ponders oft on thee is wiſe,
All fleſhly luſts ſhall he deſpiſe,
The world finds place with him no more;
The love of vain delights is o'er.
Ponder, O Man, Eternity!

Eternity! Eternity!
How long art thou, Eternity!
Who marks thee well would ſay to God,
Here, judge, burn, ſmite me with Thy rod,
Here, let me all Thy juſtice bear,
When time of grace is paſt, then ſpare!
Ponder, O Man, Eternity!

Eternity! Eternity!
How long art thou, Eternity!
Lo, I, Eternity, warn thee,
O Man, that oft thou think on me,
The ſinner's puniſhment and pain,
To them who love their God, rich gain!
Ponder, O Man, Eternity!

WULFFER. 1648.

EPIPHANY.

Ariſe, ſhine, for thy light is come, and the glory of the Lord is riſen upon thee !—FROM THE LESSON.

ALL ye Gentile lands awake!
Thou, O Salem, riſe and ſhine!
See the day-ſpring o'er you break,
Heralding a morn divine,
Telling, God hath call'd to mind
Thoſe who long in darkneſs pined.

Lo! the ſhadows flee away,
For our Light is come at length,
Brighter than all earthly day,
Source of being, life, and ſtrength!
Whoſo on this Light would gaze
Muſt forsake all evil ways.

Ah how blindly did we ſtray
Ere ſhone forth this glorious Sun,
Seeking each his ſeparate way,
Leaving Heaven unſought, unwon;
All our looks were earthwards bent,
All our ſtrength on earth was ſpent.

Earthly were our thoughts and low,
In the toils of Folly caught,

Tofs'd of Satan to and fro,
  Counting goodnefs all for nought;
By the world and flefh deceived,
Heaven's true joys we difbelieved.

Then were hidden from our eyes
  All the law and grace of God;
Small and great, the fools and wife,
  Wanting light to find the road
Leading to the heavenly life,
Wander'd loft in care and ftrife.

But the glory of the Lord
  Hath arifen on us to day!
We have feen the light outpour'd
  That muft furely drive away
All things that to night belong,
All the fad earth's woe and wrong.

Thy arifing, Lord, fhall fill
  All my thoughts in forrow's hour;
Thy arifing, Lord, fhall ftill
  All my dread of Death's dark power:
Through my fmiles and through my tears
Still Thy light, O Lord, appears.

Let me, Lord, in peace depart
  From this evil world to Thee
Where thyfelf fole Brightnefs art,
  Thou haft kept a place for me:
In the radiant city there
Crowns of light Thy faints fhall wear.

RIST. 1655.

FIRST SUNDAY AFTER EPIPHANY.

I beseech ye therefore, brethren, by the mercies of God, that ye present your bodies a living sacrifice, holy, acceptable unto God, which is your reasonable service.—FROM THE EPISTLE.

GREAT High-priest, who deigndst to be
Once the sacrifice for me,
Take this living heart of mine,
Lay it on Thy holy shrine.

Love I know accepteth nought,
Save what Thou, O Love, hast wrought;
Offer Thou my sacrifice,
Else to God it cannot rise.

Slay in me the wayward will,
Earthly sense and passion kill,
Tear self-love from out my heart,
Though it cost me bitter smart.

Kindle, mighty Love, the pyre,
Quick consume me in thy fire,
Fain were I of self bereft,
Nought but Thee within me left.

So may God the Righteous brook
On my sacrifice to look;
In whose sight no gift has worth
Save a Christ-like life on earth.

ANGELUS. 1657.

SECOND SUNDAY AFTER EPIPHANY.

Lift up your eyes unto the heavens, and look upon the earth beneath; for the heavens ſhall vaniſh away like ſmoke, and the earth ſhall wax old like a garment, and the people that dwell therein ſhall die in like manner; but my ſalvation ſhall be forever, and my righteouſneſs ſhall not be aboliſhed.—FROM THE LESSON.

GOD liveth ever!
Wherefore, Soul, deſpair thou never!
Our God is good, in every place
His love is known, His help is found,
His mighty arm, and tender grace
Bring good from ills that hem us round.
Eaſier than we think can He
Turn to joy our agony.
Soul, remember 'mid thy pains,
God o'er all for ever reigns.

God liveth ever!
Wherefore, Soul, deſpair thou never!
Say, ſhall He ſlumber, ſhall He ſleep,
Who gave the eye its power to ſee?
Shall He not hear His children weep
Who made the ear ſo wondrouſly?
God is God; He ſees and hears
All their troubles, all their tears.
Soul, forget not 'mid thy pains,
God o'er all for ever reigns.

God liveth ever!
Wherefore, Soul, deſpair thou never!
He who can earth and heaven control,
Who ſpreads the clouds o'er ſea and land,
Whoſe preſence fills the mighty Whole,
In each true heart is cloſe at hand.
Love Him, He will ſurely ſend
Help and joy that never end.
Soul, remember in thy pains,
God o'er all for ever reigns.

God liveth ever!
Wherefore, Soul, deſpair thou never!
Scarce canſt thou bear thy croſs? Then fly
To Him where only reſt is ſweet;
Thy God is great, His mercy nigh,
His ſtrength upholds the tottering feet.
Truſt Him, for His grace is ſure,
Ever doth His truth endure;
Soul, forget not in thy pains,
God o'er all for ever reigns.

God liveth ever!
O my Soul, deſpair thou never!
When ſins and follies long forgot
Upon thy tortured conſcience prey,
O come to God, and fear Him not,
His love ſhall ſweep them all away.
Pains of hell at look of His,
Change to calm content and bliſs.
Soul, forget not in thy pain,
God o'er all doth ever reign.

God liveth ever!
Wherefore, Soul, despair thou never!
Those whom the thoughtless world forsakes,
Who stand bewilder'd with their woe,
God gently to His bosom takes,
And bids them all His fulness know.
In thy sorrows' swelling flood
Own His hand who seeks thy good.
Soul, forget not in thy pains,
God o'er all for ever reigns.

God liveth ever!
Wherefore, Soul, despair thou never!
Let earth and heaven outworn with age,
Sink to the chaos whence they came;
Let angry foes against us rage,
Let hell shoot forth his fiercest flame;
Fear not Death, nor Satan's thrusts,
God defends who in Him trusts;
Soul, remember in thy pains,
God o'er all for ever reigns.

God liveth ever!
Wherefore, Soul, despair thou never!
What though thou tread with bleeding feet
A thorny path of grief and gloom,
Thy God will choose the way most meet
To lead thee heavenwards, lead thee home.
For this life's long night of sadness
He will give thee peace and gladness.
Soul, forget not in thy pains,
God o'er all for ever reigns.

ZIHN. 1682

THIRD SUNDAY AFTER EPIPHANY.

For as the rain cometh down, and the ſnow from heaven; and returneth not thither, but watereth the earth, and maketh it bring forth and bud, that it may give ſeed to the ſower, and bread to the eater: ſo ſhall my word be that goeth forth out of my mouth: it ſhall not return unto me void, but it ſhall accompliſh that which I pleaſe, and it ſhall proſper in the thing whereto I ſent it.—FROM THE LESSON.

THY Word, O Lord, like gentle dews,
Falls ſoft on hearts that pine;
Lord, to Thy garden ne'er refuſe
This heavenly balm of Thine.
Water'd from Thee
Let every tree
Bud forth and bloſſom to Thy praiſe,
And bear much fruit in after days.

Thy Word is like a flaming ſword,
A wedge that cleaveth ſtone;
Keen as a fire ſo burns Thy Word,
And pierceth fleſh and bone.
Let it go forth
O'er all the earth,
To purify all hearts within,
And ſhatter all the might of ſin.

Thy Word a wondrous guiding ſtar,
  On pilgrim hearts doth riſe,
Leads to their Lord who dwell afar,
  And makes the ſimple wiſe.
      Let not its light
      E'er ſink in night,
But ſtill in every ſpirit ſhine,
That none may miſs Thy light divine.

ANON.

FOURTH SUNDAY AFTER EPIPHANY.

And he ſaith unto them, Why are ye fearful, O ye of little faith? Then he aroſe and rebuked the winds and the ſea, and there was a great calm.—From the Gospel.

MY God! lo here before Thy face
I caſt me in the duſt;
Where is the hope of happier days,
Where is my wonted truſt?
Where are the ſunny hours I had
Ere of Thy light bereft?
Vaniſh'd is all that made me glad,
My pain alone is left.

I ſhrink with fear and ſore alarm
When threatening ills I ſee,
As in mine hour of need Thine arm
No more could ſhelter me;
As though Thou couldſt not ſee the grief
That makes my courage quail,
As though Thou wouldſt not ſend relief,
When human helpers fail.

Cannot Thy might avert e'en now
What ſeems my certain doom,
And ſtill with light and ſuccour bow
To him who weeps in gloom?

Art Thou not evermore the ſame?
  Haſt not Thyſelf revealed
In Holy Writ, that we may claim
  Thee for our ſtrength and ſhield?

O Father, compaſs me about
  With love, for I am weak;
Forgive, forgive my ſinful doubt,
  Thy pitying glance I ſeek;
For torn and anguiſh'd is my heart,
  Thou ſeeſt it, my God,
Oh ſoothe my conſcience' bitter ſmart,
  Lift off my ſorrows' load.

I know Thy thoughts are peace toward me,
  Safe am I in Thy hands,
Could I but firmly build on Thee,
  For ſure Thy counſel ſtands!
Whate'er Thy Word hath promiſed, all
  Wilt Thou full ſurely give;
Wherefore from Thee I will not fall,
  Thy Word doth make me live.

Though mountains crumble into duſt,
  Thy covenant ſtandeth faſt;
Who follows Thee in pious truſt,
  Shall reach the goal at laſt.
Though ſtrange and winding ſeem the way
  While yet on earth I dwell,
In heaven my heart ſhall gladly ſay,
  Thou, God, doſt all things well!

Take courage then, my ſoul, nor ſteep
  Thy days and nights in tears,
Soon ſhalt thou ceaſe to mourn and weep,
  Though dark are now thy fears.
He comes, He comes, the Strong to ſave,
    He comes nor tarries more,
His light is breaking o'er the wave,
  The clouds and ſtorms are o'er.

DREWES. 1797.

FIFTH SUNDAY AFTER EPIPHANY.

Oh that Thou wouldeſt rend the heavens, that Thou wouldeſt come down, that the mountains might flow down at Thy preſence . . . To make Thy name known to Thine adverſaries, that the nations may tremble at Thy preſence.—FROM THE LESSON.

AWAKE, Thou Spirit, who of old
Didſt fire the watchmen of the Church's youth,
Who faced the foe, unſhrinking, bold,
Who witneſs'd day and night the eternal truth,
Whoſe voices through the world are ringing ſtill,
And bringing hoſts to know and do Thy will!

Oh that Thy fire were kindled ſoon,
That ſwift from land to land its flame might leap!
Lord, give us but this priceleſs boon
Of faithful ſervants, fit for Thee to reap
The harveſt of the ſoul; look down and view
How great the harveſt, yet the labourers few.

Lord, let our earneſt prayer be heard,
The prayer Thy Son Himſelf hath bid us pray;
For lo! Thy children's hearts are ſtirr'd
In every land in this our darkening day,
To cry for help with fervent ſoul to Thee,
Oh hear us, Lord, and ſpeak, Thus let it be!

Oh haſte to help ere we are loſt!
Send forth evangeliſts, in ſpirit ſtrong,
Arm'd with Thy Word, a dauntleſs hoſt,
Bold to attack the rule of ancient wrong;
And let them all the earth for Thee reclaim,
To be Thy kingdom, and to know Thy name.

Would there were help within our walls!
Oh let Thy promiſed Spirit come again,
Before whom every barrier falls,
And ere the night once more ſhine forth as then!
Oh rend the heavens and make Thy preſence felt,
The chains that bind us at Thy touch would melt!

And let Thy Word have ſpeedy course,
Through every land the truth be glorified,
Till all the heathen know its force,
And gather to Thy churches far and wide;
And waken Iſrael from her ſleep, O Lord!
Thus bleſs and ſpread the conqueſts of Thy Word!

The Church's deſert paths reſtore,
And ſtumbling-blocks that long in them have lain,
Hinder Thy Word henceforth no more;
Deſtroy falſe doctrine, root out notions vain,
Set free from hirelings, let the Church and ſchool
Bloom as a garden 'neath Thy proſpering rule!

Bogatzky. 1727.

SIXTH SUNDAY AFTER EPIPHANY.

Every man that hath this hope in him purifieth himſelf even as He is pure.—From the Epistle.

PURE Eſſence! Spotleſs Fount of Light,
That fadeth never into dark!
O Thou, whoſe eyes, more clear and bright
Than noonday ſun, are quick to mark
Our ſins; lo, bare before Thy face
Lies all the deſert of my heart,
My once fair ſoul in every part
Now ſtain'd with evil foul and baſe.

Since but the pure in heart are bleſt,
With promiſed viſion of their God,
Sore fear and anguiſh fill my breaſt,
Remembering all the ways I trod;
Mourning I ſee my loſt eſtate,
And yet in faith I dare to cry,
O let my evil nature die,
Another heart in me create!

Enough, Lord, that my foe too well
Hath lured me once away from Thee;
Henceforth I know his craft how fell,
And all his deep-laid ſnares I flee.

Lord, through the Spirit whom Thy Son
 Hath bidden us in prayer to aſk,
 Arm us with might that every taſk,
Whate'er we do, in Thee be done.

Unworthy am I of Thy grace,
 So deep are my tranſgreſſions, Lord,
And yet once more I ſeek Thy face;
 My God, have mercy, nor reward
My deepen'd ſins, my follies vain;
 Reject, reject me not in wrath,
 But let Thy ſunſhine now beam forth,
And quicken me with hope again.

The Holy Spirit Thou haſt given,
 The wondrous pledge of love divine,
Who fills our hearts with joys of heaven,
 And bids us earthly toys reſign;
O let His ſeal be on my heart,
 O take Him never more away,
 Until this fleſhly houſe decay,
And Thou ſhalt bid me hence depart.

But ah! my coward ſpirit droops,
 Sick with the fear that enters in
Whene'er a ſoul to bondage ſtoops,
 And wears the ſhameful yoke of ſin;
Oh quicken with the ſtrength that flows
 From forth the Eternal Fount of Life,
 My ſoul half-fainting in the ſtrife,
And make an end of all my woes.

I cling unto Thy grace alone,
  Thy ſteadfaſt oath my only reſt;
To Thee, Heart-ſearcher, all is known
  That lieth hidden in my breaſt;
Thy gladneſs, Spirit, on me pour,
  Thy ready will my ſloth inſpire,
  So ſhall I have my heart's deſire,
And ſerve and praiſe Thee evermore.

FREYLINGHAUSEN. 1713.

SEPTUAGESIMA SUNDAY.

I therefore ſo run, not as uncertainly; so fight I, not as one that beateth the air.—FROM THE EPISTLE.

STRIVE, when thou art call'd of God,
When He draws thee by His grace,
Strive to caſt away the load
That would clog thee in the race!

Fight, though it may coſt thy life,
Storm the kingdom, but prevail,
Let not Satan's fierceſt ſtrife
Make thee, warrior, faint or quail.

Wreſtle, till through every vein
Love and ſtrength are glowing warm,
Love, that can the world diſdain,
Half-love will not bide the ſtorm.

Wreſtle, with ſtrong prayers and cries,
Think no time too much to ſpend,
Though the night be paſs'd in ſighs,
Though all day thy voice aſcend.

Haſt thou won the pearl of price,
Think not thou haſt reach'd the goal,
Conquer'd every ſin and vice
That had power to harm thy ſoul.

Gaze with mingled joy and fear
  On the refuge thou haſt found;
Know, while yet we linger here
  Perils ever hem us round.

Art thou faithful? then oppose
  Sin and wrong with all thy might;
Care not how the tempeſt blows,
  Only care to win the fight.

Art thou faithful? Wake and watch,
  Love with all thy heart Chriſt's ways,
Seek not tranſient eaſe to ſnatch,
  Look not for reward or praiſe.

Art thou faithful? Stand apart
  From all worldly hope and pleaſure,
Yonder fix your hopes and heart,
  On the heaven where lies our treaſure.

Soldiers of the Croſs, be ſtrong,
  Watch and war 'mid fear and pain,
Daily conquering woe and wrong,
  Till our King o'er earth ſhall reign!

WINKLER. 1703.

SEXAGESIMA SUNDAY.

Let them praiſe the name of the Lord, for His name alone is excellent; His glory is above the earth and heaven.—PSALM cxlviii. 13.

NOTHING fair on earth I ſee
But I ſtraightway think on Thee;
Thou art faireſt in my eyes,
Source in whom all beauty lies!

When I ſee the reddening dawn
And the golden ſun of morn,
Quickly turns this heart of mine
To Thy glorious form divine.

Oft I think upon Thy light
When the grey morn breaks the night;
Think, what glories lie in Thee,
Light of all Eternity!

When I ſee the moon ariſe
'Mid Heaven's thouſand golden eyes,
Then I think, more glorious far
Is the Maker of yon ſtar.

Or I think in ſpring's ſweet hours,
When the fields are gay with flowers,
As their varied hues I ſee,
What muſt their Creator be!

When along the brook I wander,
Or beside the fountain ponder,
Straight my thoughts take wing and mount
Up to Thee, the purest Fount.

Sweetly sings the nightingale,
Sweet the flute's soft plaintive tale,
Sweeter than their richest tone,
Is the name of Mary's Son.

Sweetly all the air is stirr'd
When the Echo's call is heard;
But no sounds my heart rejoice
Like to my Beloved's voice.

Come then, fairest Lord, appear,
Come, let me behold Thee here,
I would see Thee face to face,
On Thy proper light would gaze.

Take away these veils that blind,
Jesus, all my soul and mind;
Henceforth ever let my heart
See Thee truly as Thou art!

ANGELUS. 1657.

QUINQUAGESIMA SUNDAY.

And now abideth faith, hope, charity, theſe three; but the greateſt of theſe is charity.—FROM THE EPISTLE.

MANY a gift did Christ impart,
Nobleſt of them all is Love;
Love, a balm within the heart
That can all its pains remove;
Love, a ſtar moſt bright and pure;
Love, a gem of priceleſs worth,
Richer than man knows on earth;
Love, like beauty, ſtrong to lure;
Love, like joy, makes man her thrall,
Strong to pleaſe and conquer all.

Love can give us all things; here
Uſe and beauty cannot ſever;
Love can raiſe us to that ſphere
Whence the ſoul tends heavenwards ever;
Though one ſpake with angel tongues
Braveſt words of ſtrength and fire,
If no love his heart inſpire,
They are but as fleeting ſongs;
All his eloquence ſhall paſs,
As the noiſe of ſounding braſs.

Keen-eyed ſcience' ſearching glance,
All the wiſdom of the world,
Myſteries that the ſoul entrance,
Faith that mighty hills had hurl'd
From their ancient ſeats;—all this,
Wherein man takes moſt his pride,
Valueleſs is caſt aſide,
If the ſpirit there we miſs,
That can work from love alone,
Not from pride in what is known.

Though I laviſh'd all I have
On the poor in charity;
Though I ſhrank not from the grave,
Or unmoved the ſtake could ſee;
Though my body here were given
To the all-conſuming flame;
If my mind were ſtill the ſame,
Meeter were I not for heaven,
Till by Love my works were crown'd,
Till in Love my ſtrength were found.

Faith muſt conquer, hope muſt bloom,
As our onward way we wend,
Elſe we came not through the gloom,
But with earth they alſo end.
Thou, O Love, doſt ſtretch afar
Through the wide eternity,
And the ſoul array'd in Thee
Shines for ever as a ſtar.
Faith and hope muſt paſs away,
Thou, O Love, endureſt aye.

Come, Thou Spirit of pure Love,
Who doſt forth from God proceed,
Never from my heart remove,
Let me all Thy impulſe heed;
All that ſeeks ſelf-profit first,
Rather than another's good,
Whether foe or link'd in blood,
Let me hold ſuch thought accurſt;
And my heart henceforward be
Ruled, inſpired, O Love, by Thee!

Ernst Lange. 1711.

QUINQUAGESIMA SUNDAY.

And Jesus ſaid unto him, Receive thy ſight; thy faith hath ſaved thee. And immediately he received his ſight, and followed him, glorifying God.—FROM THE GOSPEL.

MY Saviour, what Thou didſt of old,
When Thou waſt dwelling here,
Thou doeſt yet for them, who bold
In faith to Thee draw near.
As Thou hadſt pity on the blind,
According to Thy Word,
Thou ſufferedſt me Thy grace to find,
Thy Light haſt on me pour'd.

Mourning I ſat beſide the way,
In ſightleſs gloom apart,
And ſadneſs heavy on me lay,
And longing gnaw'd my heart;
I heard the muſic of the pſalms
Thy people ſang to Thee,
I felt the waving of their palms,
And yet I could not ſee.

My pain grew more than I could bear,
Too keen my grief became,
Then I took heart in my deſpair
To call upon Thy name;

"O Son of David, ſave and heal,
As Thou ſo oft haſt done!
O deareſt Jeſus, let me feel
My load of darkneſs gone."

And ever weeping as I ſpoke
With bitter prayers and ſighs,
My ſtony heart grew ſoft and broke,
More earneſt yet my cries.
A ſudden anſwer ſtill'd my fear,
For it was ſaid to me,
"O poor blind man, be of good cheer,
Rejoice, He calleth thee."

I felt, Lord, that Thou ſtoodeſt ſtill,
Groping Thy feet I ſought,
From off me fell my old ſelf-will,
A change came o'er my thought.
Thou ſaidſt, "What is it Thou wouldſt have?"
"Lord, that I might have ſight;
To ſee Thy countenance I crave:"
"So be it, have thou Light."

And words of Thine can never fail,
My fears are paſt and o'er;
My ſoul is glad with light, the veil
Is on my heart no more.
Thou bleſſeſt me, and forth I fare
Free from my old diſgrace,
And follow on with joy where'er
Thy footſteps, Lord, I trace.

De la Mothe Fouque.

ASH WEDNESDAY.

Gather the people . . and let the priests, the ministers of the Lord, weep between the porch and the altar, and let them say, Spare Thy people, O Lord.—FROM THE PASSAGE FOR THE EPISTLE.

NOT in anger smite us, Lord,
Spare Thy people, spare!
If Thou mete us due reward
We must all despair.
Let the flood
Of Jesus' blood
Quench the flaming of Thy wrath,
That our sin enkindled hath.

Father! Thou hast patience long
With the sick and weak;
Heal us, make us brave and strong,
Words of comfort speak.
Touch my soul,
And make me whole
With Thy healing precious balm;
Ward off all would work me harm.

Weary am I, Lord, and worn
With my ceaseless pain;
Sad the heart that night and morn
Sighs for help in vain.

Wilt Thou yet
My soul forget,
Waiting anxiously for Thee
In the cave of misery?

Hence, ye foes! God hears my prayer
From His holy place;
Once again with hope I dare
Come before His face.
Satan flee,
Hell touch not me;
God hath given me power o'er all,
Who once mock'd and sought my fall.

ALBINUS. 1652.

FIRST SUNDAY IN LENT.

Then was Jesus led up of the Spirit into the wilderness to be tempted of the devil. And he fasted forty days and forty nights.—FROM THE GOSPEL.

AM I a stranger here, on earth alone,
When shall my weary days be past and gone?
When shall I find some respite, some relief
From this unsleeping pain, this haunting grief?

The joyful sun another morning brings,
I only wake to feel care's piercing stings;
The soft moon comes with silent night and sleep,
And bringeth nought to me but time to weep.

My heart and conscience sorely wounded lie,
Struck by the arrows of Thy wrath, Most High!
From morn till eventide where'er I flee,
I find no hiding-place, great God, from Thee!

O Lord, be not so strict to mark my crimes!
Great God, dost Thou remember yet those times
Of foolish thoughtlessness, when blind and young
My heart to this world's vain delights still clung?

Wilt Thou then alway bear my sins in mind?
What offering, what atonement can I find!

Nought have I of mine own but ſin and wrong,
Mercy and love, O Lord, to Thee belong!

On therefore leave me not the wretched prey
Of thoſe who ſeek to take my life away!
Yet though with ſtreaming eyes to Thee I cry,
No anſwering voice comes from Thy throne on high

Vain are my tears and prayers, vain all my woe,
While Thou doſt fight againſt me as a foe;
The zeal of Thy juſt anger and Thy might
Have plunged my ſoul in blackeſt depths of night.

I ſit alone; with tears I bathe my cheeks,
With bitter ſighs and groans my ſpirit ſeeks
For Him, who veils behind the clouds His face,
And hears not, as of old in happier days.

Oh that I had a dove's ſwift wings! I'd fly
Away to ſome far mountain, lone and high;
Yet could I not eſcape His mighty hand
Before whom all things bare and open ſtand.

Nay, rather let me ſuffer all His will,
Though His fierce anger beat upon me ſtill,
A willing heart and patient mind, O God!
I bring to Thy ſevere but righteous rod.

Much have I ſinn'd, I periſh utterly
If my miſdeeds be all avenged of Thee;
Yet, Lord of Hoſts, doth not Thy Word proclaim,
The Merciful is Thy moſt glorious name!

Raisner. 1678.

SECOND SUNDAY IN LENT.

And the disciples said, Send her away, for she crieth after us; . . . But He said, Great is thy faith, be it unto thee even as thou wilt.—FROM THE GOSPEL.

I WILL not let Thee go; Thou Help in
time of need!
Heap ill on ill
I trust Thee still,
E'en when it seems as Thou wouldst slay indeed!
Do as Thou wilt with me,
I yet will cling to Thee,
Hide Thou Thy face, yet Help in time of need,
I will not let Thee go!

I will not let Thee go; should I forsake my bliss?
No, Lord, Thou'rt mine,
And I am Thine,
Thee will I hold when all things else I miss
Though dark and sad the night,
Joy cometh with Thy light,
O Thou my Sun; should I forsake my bliss?
I will not let Thee go!

I will not let Thee go, my God, my Life, my Lord!
Not Death can tear
Me from His care,
Who for my sake His soul in death outpour'd.

Thou diedst for love to me,
I say in love to Thee,
E'en when my heart shall break, my God, my Life, my Lord,
I will not let Thee go!

DESZLER. 1692.

THIRD SUNDAY IN LENT.

Awake, thou that ſleepeſt, and ariſe from the dead, and Chriſt ſhall give thee light.—FROM THE EPISTLE.

AWAKE, O man, and from thee ſhake
This heavy ſleep of ſin!
Soon ſhall the Higheſt vengeance take,
Soon ſhall His wrath begin
To ſmite the wretched ſinner home;
In awful terrors He ſhall come,
To mete to all on earth their due reward,
Only the righteous ſpares our angry Lord.

Come then, ye ſinners, great and ſmall,
Weeping and mourning ſore,
Low down before His footſtool fall,
And vow to ſin no more.
In faith and godlineſs array
Your ſouls againſt that final day,
So ſhall ye 'ſcape His wrath, and bleſſed die,
Heirs of the kingdom with your Lord on high.

O lay to heart this wondrous thought,
Through what ſore agony
And death was your redemption bought,
And to your Saviour flee

Ere yet too late; the world diſown,
And fix your love on Chriſt alone,
And do His will; for at the final doom,
Who here diſhonour'd Him ſhall wrath conſume.

Turn Thou us, and we ſhall be turn'd;
Thou broughteſt back of old
Thy ſtraying people, when they yearn'd
After their proper fold:
Even ſo, forgive what we have done,
Accept us in Thy bleſſed Son,
Thy Holy Spirit ever be our guide,
That we may ſpread Thy praiſes far and wide!

CRASSELIUS. 1697.

FOURTH SUNDAY IN LENT.

Grant we beſeech Thee, Almighty God, that we, who for our evil deeds do worthily deſerve to be puniſhed, by the comfort of Thy grace may mercifully be relieved; through our Lord and Saviour, Jeſus Chriſt.—FROM THE COLLECT.

HERE, O my God, I caſt me at Thy feet,
Ready to ſuffer what Thou thinkeſt meet;
Yet look on me, great God, with pitying eyes,
Reward me not for mine iniquities!

Too oft, alas! my heart hath loved to ſtray
Downward along Sin's broad and eaſy way;
And worldly pride, and carnal luſts moſt foul
Were ſhameleſs cheriſh'd in my inmoſt ſoul.

Thy Majeſty have I offended, Lord,
And ſet at nought Thy law, Thy holy Word;
I had not learnt Thy righteous wrath to dread,
Nor ſaw the vengeance gathering o'er my head.

O wretched man, what evil have I wrought!
Now in the ſnares of Sin a captive caught,
I learn, O Sin, how fell and keen thy ſmart!
O wrath of God, how terrible thou art!

Is there no way, can I no helper find,
Who can these heavy chains of sin unbind?
Can man nor creature show me any place,
Where I may flee and hide me from God's face?

Nay, I must flee to God Himself, from whom
Our life and help, our hope and safety come;
What all the world must unaccomplish'd leave,
Thou, for Thou art Almighty, canst achieve.

Think on the covenant Thou hast never broken,
Think on the steadfast oath Thyself hast spoken;
Know that I am a God, Thy promise saith,
Who hath no pleasure in a sinner's death.

Then let the arms of love be round me thrown,
Have pity on me, hear my bitter moan,
Call back Thy sheep, that wandering far astray,
Was lost in sin, nor knew its homeward way.

Grant me to rule my inner life aright,
And act and speak as ever in Thy sight,
A friend to all true virtue, but a foe
To all Thou hatest, sins and follies low.

Thou Merciful! what thanks and praise shall be
For Thy great goodness offer'd unto Thee,
As 'tis most meet; while here my days I spend,
And yonder in the world that shall not end!

Anon.

FIFTH SUNDAY IN LENT.

Out of the depths have I called unto Thee, O Lord. Lord, hear my voice. If Thou, Lord, wilt be extreme to mark what is done amiſs, O Lord, who may abid it?—PSALM cxxx. 1, 3.

OUT of the depths I cry to Thee,
Lord God! oh hear my prayer
Incline a gracious ear to me,
And bid me not deſpair:
If Thou remembereſt each miſdeed,
If each ſhould have its rightful meed,
Lord, who ſhall ſtand before Thee?

Lord, through Thy love alone we gain
The pardon of our ſin;
The ſtricteſt life is but in vain,
Our works can nothing win,
That none ſhould boaſt himſelf of aught,
But own in fear Thy grace hath wrought
What in him ſeemeth righteous.

Wherefore my hope is in the Lord,
My works I count but duſt,
I build not there, but on His word,
And in His goodneſs truſt.
Up to His care myſelf I yield,
He is my tower, my rock, my ſhield,
And for His help I tarry.

And though it tarry till the night,
And round again to morn,
My heart ſhall ne'er miſtruſt Thy might,
Nor count itſelf forlorn.
Do thus, O ye of Iſrael's ſeed,
Ye of the Spirit born indeed,
Wait for your God's appearing.

Though great our ſins and ſore our wounds,
And deep and dark our fall,
His helping mercy hath no bounds,
His love ſurpaſseth all.
Our truſty loving Shepherd He,
Who ſhall at laſt ſet Iſrael free
From all their ſin and ſorrow.

LUTHER. 1524.

PALM SUNDAY.

And the multitudes that went before, and that followed, cried, ſaying, Hoſanna to the Son of David; bleſſed is he that cometh in the name of the Lord; Hoſanna in the higheſt.—MATT. xxi. 9.

HOSANNA to the Son of David! Raiſe
Triumphal arches to His praiſe,
For Him prepare a throne
Who comes at laſt to Zion—to His own!
Strew palms around, make plain and ſtraight the way,
For Him who His triumphal entry holds to-day!

Hoſanna! Welcome above all Thou art!
Make ready each to lay his heart
Low down before His feet!
Come, let us haſten forth our Lord to meet,
And bid Him enter in at Zion's gates,
Where thouſand-voiced welcome on His coming waits.

Hoſanna! Prince of Peace and Lord of Might!
We hail Thee Conqueror in the fight.
All Thou with toil haſt won,
Shall be our booty when the battle's done.
Thy right hand ever hath the rule and ſway,
Thy kingdom ſtandeth faſt when all things elſe decay.

Hoſanna! beſt-beloved and noble Gueſt!
Who made us by Thy high beheſt
Heirs of Thy realm with Thee.
O let us therefore never weary be
To ſtand and ſerve before Thy righteous throne,
We know no king but Thee, rule Thou o'er us alone

Hoſanna! Come, the time draws on apace,
We long Thy mercy to embrace;
This ſervant's form can ne'er
Conceal the majeſty Thy acts declare:
Too well art Thou here in Thy Zion known,
Who art the Son of God, and yet art David's Son.

Hoſanna! Lord, be Thou our help and friend,
Thy aid to us in mercy ſend,
That each may bring his ſoul
An offering unto Thee, unſtain'd and whole.
Thou wilt have none for Thy diſciples, Lord,
But who obey in truth, not only hear Thy word.

Hoſanna! Let us in Thy footſteps tread,
Nor that ſad Mount of Olives dread
Where we muſt weep and watch,
Until the far-off ſong of joy we catch
From Heaven our Bethphage, where we ſhall ſing
Hoſanna in the higheſt to our God and King!

Hoſanna! Let us ſound it far and wide!
Enter Thou in and here abide,
Thou Bleſſed of the Lord!

Why ſtandeſt Thou without, why roam'ſt
abroad?
Hoſanna! Make Thy home with us for ever!
Thou comeſt, Lord! and nought us from Thy love
ſhall ſever.
Hallelujah.

SCHMOLCK. 1704.

MONDAY IN PASSION WEEK.

And when He was come near, He beheld the city, and wept over it.—LUKE xix. 41.

THOU weepeſt o'er Jeruſalem,
Lord Jeſus, bitter tears;
But deepeſt comfort lies in them
For us, whoſe ſins have fill'd our ſouls with fears:
Since that they tell,
When ſinners turn to Thee Thou lov'ſt it well,
And ſurely wilt efface, of Thy unbounded grace,
All the miſdeeds that on our conſcience dwell.

When God's juſt wrath and anger burn
Againſt me for my ſin,
To theſe ſad tears of Thine I turn,
And watching them freſh hope and courage win.
For God doth prize
Theſe drops ſo greatly, that before His eyes
Who ſprinkles o'er his ſoul with them is clean and whole,
And from his ſorrows' depth new joy ſhall riſe.

Earth is the home of tears and woe,
Where we muſt often weep,
Fighting the world our mighty foe,
Whoſe enmity to Thee doth never ſleep.

My heart is torn
Afresh each day by her fierce rage and scorn,
But in my saddest hours, I think upon those showers
That tell how Thou hast all our sorrows borne.

Thou countest up my tears and sighs;
E'en were they numberless.
Not one is hidden from Thine eyes,
Thou ne'er forgettest me in my distress,
But when they rain
Before Thee, Thou dost quickly turn again,
Hast pity on my woe, and makest me to know
What sweetest joy lies hid in sorest pain.

We sow in tears; but let us keep
Our faith in God, and trust Him still,
Yonder our harvest we shall reap,
Where gladness every heart and mouth shall fill.
Such joy is there
No mortal tongue its glory can declare,
A joy that shall endure, changeless and deep and pure
That shall be ours, if here the cross we bear.

O Christ, I thank Thee for Thy tears;
Those tears have won for me
That I shall wear, through endless years,
A crown of joy before my God and Thee
All weeping o'er,
Up to Thy chosen saints I once shall soar,
And there Thy pity praise, in more befitting lays,
Thou Glory of Thy Church, for evermore.

HEERMANN. 1630.

TUESDAY IN PASSION WEEK.

By the which will we are ſanctified, through the offering of the body of Jeſus Chriſt once for all.—HEB. x. 10.

LORD! Thy death and paſſion give
Strength and comfort at my need,
Every hour while here I live
On Thy love my ſoul ſhall feed.
Doth ſome evil thought upſtart?
Lo, Thy croſs defends my heart,
Shows the peril, and I ſhrink
Back from loitering on the brink.

Doth my carnal nature yearn
After wanton joys? again
Quickly to Thy croſs I turn,
And her voice is heard in vain.
Cometh ſtrong temptation's hour,
When my foe puts forth his power?
Shelter'd by this holy ſhield,
Soon I drive him from the field.

Would the world my ſteps entice
To yon wide and level road,
Fill'd with mirth and pleaſant vice?
Lord, I think upon the load

Thou didst once for me endure,
And I fly all thoughts impure;
Thinking on Thy bitter pains,
Hush'd in prayer my heart remains.

Yes, Thy cross hath power to heal
  All the wounds of sin and strife,
Lost in Thee my heart doth feel
  Sudden warmth and nobler life.
In my saddest, darkest grief,
Let Thy sweetness bring relief,
Thou who camest but to save,
Thou who fearest not the grave!

Lord, in Thee I place my trust,
  Thou art my defence and tower;
Death Thou treadest in the dust,
  O'er my soul he hath no power.
That I may have part in Thee
Help and save and comfort me,
Give me of Thy grace and might,
Resurrection, life and light.

Fount of Good, within me dwell,
  For the peace Thy presence sheds,
Keeps us safe in conflict fell,
  Charms the pain from dying beds.
Hide me safe within Thine arm,
Where no foe can hurt or harm;
Whoso, Lord, in Thee doth rest,
He hath conquer'd, he is blest.

Heermann. 1644.

WEDNESDAY IN PASSION WEEK.

Now once in the end of the world hath He appeared, to put away ſin by the ſacrifice of Himſelf.—FROM THE EPISTLE.

WHEN ſorrow and remorſe
Prey at my heart, to Thee
I look, who on the holy croſs
Waſt ſlain for me.
Ah Lord, Thy precious blood was ſpilt
For me, O moſt unworthy,
To take away my guilt.

Oh wonder paſt belief!
Behold the Maſter ſpares
His ſervants, and ſore pain and grief
For them He bears.
God ſtoopeth from His throne on high,
For me His guilty creature,
He deigns as man to die.

Though countleſs were the ſins,
That weigh'd me to the duſt,
Chriſt's death for me the favour wins
Of God moſt juſt.
His precious blood my debts hath paid,
Of hell and all its torments
I am no more afraid.

My heart is fill'd with ruth,
Thinking on all Thou'st borne,
How mighty love and tender truth
Were crown'd with thorn.
In songs of thanks I'll spend my breath
For Thy sad cry, Thy sufferings,
Thy wrongs, Thy guiltless death.

Thy Passion, Lord, inspires
My spirit day by day,
With strength from all low dark desires
To flee away.
This thought I fain would cherish most,
What pain my soul's redemption
To Thee, O Saviour, cost.

Whate'er the burden be,
The cross upon me laid,
Or want or shame, I look to Thee,
Be Thou my aid.
Give patience, give me strength to take
Thee for my bright example,
And all the world forsake.

Let me to others do,
As Thou hast done to me,
Love them with love unfeign'd and true,
Their servant be
Of willing heart, nor seek my own,
But as Thou, Lord, hast helped us,
From purest love alone.

And let Thy ſorrows cheer
My ſoul when I depart;
Give ſtrength to caſt away all fear,
And tell my heart
That ſince my truſt is in Thy grace,
Thou wilt accept me yonder,
Where I ſhall ſee Thy face.

GESENIUS. 1646.

THURSDAY IN PASSION WEEK.

Pilate therefore, willing to releafe Jefus, fpake again to them. But they cried, faying, Crucify him, crucify him. And he faid unto them the third time, Why, what evil hath he done?—FROM THE GOSPEL.

ALAS, dear Lord, what evil haft Thou done,
That fuch fharp fentence from Thy Judge hath won?
What are His crimes, and what the guilt, oh tell,
Wherein He fell?

They fcourge Him, crown Him with a crown of thorn,
They fmite His face, with bitter mock and fcorn,
They give Him gall to drink, they pierce His fide,
The Crucified!

Whence come thefe forrows, whence this cruel woe?
It was my fins that ftruck the fatal blow;
Mine were the wrath and anguifh, deareft Lord,
On Thee outpour'd.

What ftrangeft punifhment! The Shepherd good
For erring fheep here pours His own heart's blood,
The fervants' debts are on the Mafter laid,
Who all hath paid.

From head to foot was there no ſpot in me
Unſcarr'd by ſin, from taint of evil free;
My ſins had weigh'd me down that I ſhould dwell,
For aye in Hell.

Oh wondrous love, love that no meaſure knows,
That brought Thee, Chriſt, to drink this cup of woes!
Full of the world's vain joys and hopes was I,
While Thou muſt die!

O mighty King! mighty beyond all time!
Fain would I ſound Thy praiſe through every clime!
A gift were meet for Thee, my anxious thought
Long time hath ſought.

But human wiſdom ſearches, Lord, in vain
To find aught like Thy pity, or Thy pain.
How ſhall my works, though toiling day and night,
Thy love requite?

Yet have I somewhat that my Lord can pleaſe;
I can renounce ſweet ſins and ſelfiſh eaſe,
And quench the unhallow'd fires that back would lure
To thoughts impure.

But ſince my ſtrength, alas, will ne'er prevail
My ſtrong deſires upon the croſs to nail,
Oh let Thy Spirit rule my heart, who leads
To all good deeds.

Then ſhall Thy mercy fill my every thought;
I love Thee ſo, the world to me is nought.
My ſole endeavour, Lord, is to fulfil
Thy holy will.

My all I riſk to magnify Thy name,
No croſs ſhall daunt me, no reproach or ſhame;
Man's fierceſt threats I will not lay to heart,
Nor Death's worſt ſmart.

In truth my ſacrifice is nothing worth,
Yet Thou in mercy wilt not caſt it forth;
Thou'lt put me not to ſhame, but for love's ſake
My offering take.

Lord Jeſus, once on high amongſt Thine own,
Shall I ſtand crown'd with light before Thy throne;
Where ſweeteſt hymns are ever ringing round
My voice ſhall ſound.

Heermann. 1630.

GOOD FRIDAY.

Morning.

He was wounded for our tranſgreſſions, He was bruiſed for our iniquities: the chaſtiſement of our peace was upon Him, and with His ſtripes we are healed.—From the Lesson.

Ah wounded Head! Muſt Thou
Endure ſuch ſhame and ſcorn!
The blood is trickling from Thy brow
Pierced by the crown of thorn.
Thou who waſt crown'd on high
With light and majeſty,
In deep diſhonour here muſt die,
Yet here I welcome Thee!

Thou noble countenance!
All earthly lights are pale
Before the brightneſs of that glance,
At which a world ſhall quail.
How is it quench'd and gone!
Thoſe gracious eyes how dim!
Whence grew that cheek ſo pale and wan?
Who dared to ſcoff at Him?

All lovely hues of life,
That glow'd on lip and cheek,
Have vaniſhed in that awful ſtrife;
The Mighty One is weak.

Pale Death has won the day,
He triumphs in this hour
When Strength and Beauty fade away,
And yield them to his power.

Ah Lord, Thy woes belong,
Thy cruel pains, to me,
The burden of my ſin and wrong
Hath all been laid on Thee.
Look on me where I kneel,
Wrath were my rightful lot,
One glance of love oh let me feel!
Redeemer, ſpurn me not!

My Guardian, own me Thine;
Thy lamb, O Shepherd, lead!
What richeſt bleſſings, Source Divine,
Daily from Thee proceed!
How oft Thy mouth has fed
My ſoul with angels' food,
How oft Thy Spirit o'er me ſhed
His ſtores of heavenly good!

Ah would that I could ſhare
Thy croſs, Thy bitter woes!
All true delight lies hidden there,
Thence all true comfort flows.
Ah well were it for me
Could I here end my ſtrife,
And die upon the croſs with Thee,
Who art my Life of life!

O Jeſus, deareſt Friend,
My ſoul is all o'erfraught
With thanks, when pondering to what end
Thou haſt the battle fought.
Oh let me faithful keep,
As Thou art true to me,
So ſhall my laſt cold deathly ſleep
Be but a reſt in Thee.

Yes, when I hence muſt go,
Go not Thou, Chriſt, from me;
When Death has ſtruck the mortal blow,
Bear Thou mine agony.
When heart and ſpirit ſink,
O'erwhelm'd with dark diſmay,
Come Thou who ne'er from pain didſt ſhrink,
And chaſe my fears away.

Come to me ere I die,
My comfort and my ſhield;
And gazing on Thy croſs can I
Calmly my ſpirit yield.
When life is well-nigh paſt,
My darkening eyes ſhall dwell
On Thee, my heart ſhall hold Thee faſt;
Who dieth thus, dies well.

Paul Gerhardt. 1659.

GOOD FRIDAY.

Evening.

But God commendeth his love toward us, in that, while we were yet ſinners, Chriſt died for us.—Rom. v. 8.

THOU Holieſt Love, whom moſt I love,
Who art my long'd-for only bliſs,
Whom tendereſt pity erſt did move
To fathom woe and death's abyſs;
Thou who didſt ſuffer for my good,
And die my guilty debts to pay,
Thou Lamb of God, whoſe precious blood
Can take a world's miſdeeds away;

Thou who didſt bear the agony
That made e'en Thy ſtrong ſpirit quail,
Yet ever yearneſt ſtill for me
With longing love that ne'er ſhall fail;
'Twas Thou waſt willing, Thou alone,
To bear the righteous wrath of God;
Thy death hath ſtill'd it, elſe had none
Found ſhelter from its awful load.

O Love, who with unflinching heart
Didſt bear all worſt diſgrace and ſhame;
O Love, who mid the keeneſt ſmart
Of dying pangs wert ſtill the ſame;

Who didſt Thy changeleſs virtue prove
E'en with Thy lateſt parting breath,
And ſpakeſt words of gentleſt love
When ſoul and body ſank in death;

O Love, through ſorrows manifold
Haſt Thou betroth'd me as a bride,
By ceaſeleſs gifts, by love untold,
Haſt bound me ever to Thy ſide.
Oh let the weary ache, the ſmart,
Of life's long tale of pain and loſs,
Be gently ſtill'd within my heart
At thought of Thee, and of Thy croſs!

O Love, who gav'ſt Thy life for me,
And won an everlaſting good
Through Thy ſore anguiſh on the tree,
I ever think upon Thy blood;
I ever thank Thy ſacred wounds,
Thou wounded Love, Thou Holieſt,
But moſt when life is near its bounds,
And in Thy boſom ſafe I reſt.

O Love, who unto death haſt grieved
For this cold heart, unworthy Thine,
Whom the cold grave and death received,
I thank Thee for that grief divine.
I give Thee thanks that Thou didſt die
To win eternal life for me,
To bring ſalvation from on high;
Oh draw me up through love to Thee!

Angelus. 1657.

EASTER EVEN.

And Joſeph wrapped the body in a clean linen cloth, and laid it in his own new tomb, which he had hewn out in the rock.—FROM THE GOSPEL.

REST of the weary! Thou
Thyſelf art reſting now,
Where lowly in Thy ſepulchre Thou lieſt:
From out her deathly ſleep
My ſoul doth ſtart, to weep
So ſad a wonder, that Thou Saviour dieſt!

Thy bitter anguiſh o'er,
To this dark tomb they bore
Thee, Life of life—Thee, Lord of all creation!
The hollow rocky cave
Muſt ſerve Thee for a grave,
Who waſt Thyſelf the Rock of our Salvation!

O Prince of Life! I know
That when I too lie low,
Thou wilt at laſt my ſoul from death awaken;
Wherefore I will not ſhrink
From the grave's awful brink;
The heart that truſts in Thee ſhall ne'er be ſhaken.

To me the darkſome tomb
Is but a narrow room,
Where I may reſt in peace from ſorrow free.
Thy death ſhall give me power
To cry in that dark hour,
O Death, O Grave, where is your victory?

The grave can nought deſtroy,
Only the fleſh can die,
And e'en the body triumphs o'er decay:
Cloth'd by Thy wondrous might
In robes of dazzling light,
This fleſh ſhall burſt the grave at that laſt Day.

My Jeſus, day by day,
Help me to watch and pray,
Beſide the tomb where in my heart Thou'rt laid.
Thy bitter death ſhall be
My conſtant memory,
My guide at laſt into Death's awful ſhade.

S. FRANCK. 1711.

EASTER DAY.

MORNING.

Chriſt being raiſed from the dead dieth no more: death hath no more dominion over him.—FROM THE ANTHEM.

IN the bonds of Death He lay,
Who for our offence was ſlain,
But the Lord is riſen to-day,
Chriſt hath brought us life again
Wherefore let us all rejoice,
Singing loud with cheerful voice
Hallelujah!

Of the ſons of men was none
Who could break the bonds of Death,
Sin this miſchief dire had done,
Innocent was none on earth,
Wherefore Death grew ſtrong and bold,
Would all men in his priſon hold,
Hallelujah!

Jeſus Chriſt, God's only Son,
Came at laſt our foe to ſmite,
All our ſins away hath done,
Done away Death's power and right,
Only the form of Death is left,
Of his ſting he is bereft;
Hallelujah.

That was a wondrous war I trow,
When Life and Death together fought,
But Life hath triumph'd o'er his foe,
Death is mock'd and ſet at nought;
'Tis even as the Scripture ſaith,
Chriſt through death has conquer'd Death.
Hallelujah.

The rightful Paſchal Lamb is He,
On whom alone we all muſt live,
Who to death upon the tree,
Himſelf in wondrous love did give.
Faith ſtrikes his blood upon the door,
Death ſees, and dares not harm us more.
Hallelujah.

Let us keep high feſtival,
On this moſt bleſſed day of days,
When God His mercy ſhow'd to all!
Our Sun is riſen with brighteſt rays,
And our dark hearts rejoice to ſee
Sin and night before him flee.
Hallelujah.

To the ſupper of the Lord,
Gladly will we come to-day,
The word of peace is now reſtored,
The old leaven is put away.
Chriſt will be our food alone,
Faith no life but His doth own.
Hallelujah.

Luther. 1524.

EASTER DAY.

Evening.

If ye then be risen with Christ, seek those things which are above, where Christ sitteth on the right hand of God.—From the Epistle.

O GLORIOUS Head, Thou livest now!
Let us Thy members share Thy life;
Canst Thou behold their need, nor bow
To raise Thy children from the strife
With self and sin, with death and dark distress,
That they may live to Thee in holiness?

Earth knows Thee not, but evermore
Thou livest in Paradise, in peace;
Thither my soul would also soar,
Let me from all the creatures cease:
Dead to the world, but to Thy Spirit known,
I live to Thee, O Prince of life, alone.

Break through my bonds whate'er it cost,
What is not Thine within me slay,
Give me the lot I covet most,
To rise as Thou hast risen to-day.
Nought can I do, a slave to death I pine,
Work Thou in me, O Power and Life Divine!

Work Thou in me, and heavenward guide
  My thoughts and wishes, that my heart
Waver no more nor turn aside,
  But fix for ever where Thou art.
Thou art not far from us; who love Thee well,
While yet on earth in heaven with Thee may dwell.

TERSTEEGEN. 1731.

MONDAY IN EASTER WEEK.

And they told what things were done in the way, and how He was known to them in breaking of bread. And as they thus ſpake, Jeſus himſelf ſtood in the midſt of them, and ſaith unto them, Peace be unto you. — From the Gospel.

WELCOME Thou victor in the ſtrife,
Welcome from out the cave!
To-day we triumph in Thy life
Around Thine empty grave.

Our enemy is put to ſhame,
His ſhort-lived triumph o'er;
Our God is with us, we exclaim,
We fear our foe no more.

The dwellings of the juſt reſound
With ſongs of victory;
For in their midſt Thou, Lord, art found,
And bringeſt peace with Thee.

O ſhare with us the ſpoils, we pray,
Thou diedſt to achieve;
We meet within Thy houſe to-day
Our portion to receive:

And let Thy conquering banner wave
  O'er hearts Thou makeſt free,
And point the path that from the grave
  Leads heavenwards up to Thee.

We bury all our ſin and crime
  Deep in our Saviour's tomb,
And ſeek the treaſure there, that time
  Nor change can e'er conſume.

We die with Thee; oh let us live
  Henceforth to Thee aright;
The bleſſings Thou haſt died to give,
  Be daily in our ſight.

Fearleſs we lay us in the tomb,
  And ſleep the night away,
If Thou art there to break the gloom,
  And call us back to day.

Death hurts us not; his power is gone,
  And pointleſs all his darts;
God's favour now on us hath ſhone,
  Joy filleth all our hearts.

SCHMOLCK. 1712.

TUESDAY IN EASTER WEEK.

I know that my Redeemer liveth . . and though after my ſkin worms deſtroy this body, yet in my fleſh ſhall I ſee God.—JOB xix. 25, 26.

For this corruptible muſt put on incorruption, and this mortal muſt put on immortality.—FROM THE LESSON.

JESUS my Redeemer lives,
Chriſt my truſt is dead no more;
In the ſtrength this knowledge gives
Shall not all my fears be o'er;
Calm, though death's long night be fraught
Still with many an anxious thought?

Jeſus my Redeemer lives,
And His life I once ſhall ſee;
Bright the hope this promiſe gives,
Where He is I too ſhall be.
Shall I fear then? Can the Head
Riſe and leave the members dead?

Cloſe to Him my ſoul is bound
In the bonds of Hope enclaſp'd;
Faith's ſtrong hand this hold hath found,
And the Rock hath firmly graſp'd.

Death ſhall ne'er my ſoul remove
From her refuge in Thy love.

I ſhall ſee Him with theſe eyes,
  Him whom I ſhall ſurely know;
Not another ſhall I riſe,
  With His love this heart ſhall glow;
Only there ſhall diſappear
Weakneſs in and round me here.

Ye who ſuffer, ſigh, and moan,
  Freſh and glorious there ſhall reign;
Earthly here the ſeed is ſown,
  Heavenly it ſhall riſe again;
Natural here the death we die,
Spiritual our life on high.

Body, be thou of good cheer,
  In thy Saviour's care rejoice,
Give not place to gloom and fear,
  Dead; thou yet ſhalt know His voice,
When the final trump is heard,
And the deaf cold grave is ſtirr'd.

Laugh to ſcorn then death and hell,
  Laugh to ſcorn the gloomy grave;
Caught into the air to dwell
  With the Lord who comes to ſave,
We ſhall trample on our foes,
Mortal weakneſs, fear and woes.

Only ſee ye that your heart,
  Riſe betimes from earthly luſt,
Would ye there with Him have part,
  Here obey your Lord and truſt.
Fix your hearts beyond the ſkies,
Whither ye yourſelves would riſe.

LOUISA HENRIETTA,
Electreſs of Brandenburg. 1653.

FIRST SUNDAY AFTER EASTER.

God hath given to us eternal life, and this life is in His Son.—From the Epistle.

WHAT had I been if Thou wert not?
What were I now if Thou wert gone?
Anguiſh and fear were then my lot,
In this wide world I ſtood alone;
Whate'er I loved were ſafe no more,
The future were a dark abyſs,
To whom could I my ſorrows pour,
If Thee my laden heart ſhould miſs?

But when Thou mak'ſt Thy preſence felt,
And when the ſoul hath graſp'd Thee right
How faſt the dreary ſhadows melt
Beneath Thy warm and living light:
In Thee I find a nobler birth,
A glory o'er the world I ſee,
And Paradiſe returns to earth,
And blooms again for us in Thee.

Thou ſtrong and loving Son of Man,
Redeemer from the bonds of ſin,
'Tis Thou the living ſpark doſt fan
That ſets my heart on fire within.

Thou openest heaven once more to men,
  The soul's true home, Thy kingdom, Lord,
And I can trust and hope again,
  And feel myself akin to God.

Brethren, go forth beside all ways,
  The wanderer greet with outstretch'd hand,
And call him back who darkly strays,
  And bid him join our gladsome band.
That Heaven hath stoop'd to earth below,
  Proclaim the glad news everywhere,
That all may learn our faith and know
  They too may find an entrance there.

NOVALIS. About 1795.

SECOND SUNDAY AFTER EASTER.

Jesus said, I am the Good Shepherd: the Good Shepherd giveth His life for His sheep.—FROM THE GOSPEL.

LOVING Shepherd, kind and true,
Wilt Thou not in pity come
To Thy lamb? As shepherds do,
Bear me in Thy bosom home;
Take me hence from earth's annoy
To Thy home of endless joy.

See how I have gone astray
In this earthly wilderness;
Come and take me hence away
To Thy flock who dwell in bliss,
And Thy glory, Lord, behold,
Safe within Thy heavenly fold.

For I fain would gaze on Thee,
With the lambs to whom 'tis given
That they feed from danger free,
In the happy fields of heaven;
Praising Thee, all terrors o'er,
Never can they wander more.

Here I live in sore distress,
Careful, timid, every hour;

For my foes around me prefs,
  Hem me in with craft and power:
Not one moment fafe can be,
Lord, Thy lamb away from Thee.

O Lord Jefus, let me not
  'Mid the ravening wolves e'er fall,
Help me as a fhepherd ought,
  That I may efcape them all;
Bear me homeward in Thy breaft,
To Thy fold of endlefs reft.

ANGELUS. 1657.

THIRD SUNDAY AFTER EASTER.

And ye now therefore have ſorrow; but I will ſee you again, and your heart ſhall rejoice, and your joy no man taketh from you.—FROM THE GOSPEL.

COMETH ſunſhine after rain,
After mourning joy again,
After heavy bitter grief
Dawneth ſurely ſweet relief;
And my ſoul, who from her height
Sank to realms of woe and night,
Wingeth now to heaven her flight.

He, whom this world dares not face,
Hath refreſh'd me with His grace,
And His mighty hand unbound
Chains of hell about me wound;
Quicker, ſtronger, leaps my blood,
Since His mercy, like a flood,
Pour'd o'er all my heart for good.

Bitter anguiſh have I borne,
Keen regret my heart hath torn,
Sorrow dimm'd my weeping eyes,
Satan blinded me with lies;
Yet at laſt am I ſet free,
Help, protection, love, to me
Once more true companions be.

Ne'er was left a helpless prey,
Ne'er with shame was turn'd away,
He who gave himself to God,
And on Him had cast his load.
    Who in God his hope hath placed
    Shall not life in pain outwaste,
    Fullest joy he yet shall taste.

Though to-day may not fulfil
All thy hopes, have patience still;
For perchance to-morrow's sun
Sees thy happier days begun.
    As God willeth march the hours,
    Bringing joy at last in showers,
    And whate'er we ask'd is ours.

When my heart was vex'd with care,
Fill'd with fears well nigh despair;
When with watching many a night,
On me fell pale sickness' blight;
    When my courage fail'd me fast,
    Camest Thou, my God, at last,
    And my woes were quickly past.

Now as long as here I roam,
On this earth have house and home,
Shall this wondrous gleam from Thee
Shine through all my memory.
    To my God I yet will cling,
    All my life the praises sing
    That from thankful hearts outspring.

Every ſorrow, every ſmart,
That the Eternal Father's heart
Hath appointed me of yore,
Or hath yet for me in ſtore,
    As my life flows on I'll take
    Calmly, gladly for His ſake,
    No more faithleſs murmurs make.

I will meet diſtreſs and pain,
I will greet e'en death's dark reign,
I will lay me in the grave,
With a heart ſtill glad and brave.
    Whom the Strongeſt doth defend,
    Whom the Higheſt counts His ſriend,
    Cannot periſh in the end.

PAUL GERHARDT. 1659.

FOURTH SUNDAY AFTER EASTER.

It is expedient for you that I go away, for if I go not away, the Comforter will not come unto you.—FROM THE GOSPEL.

O HOLY Ghoſt! Thou fire Divine!
From higheſt heaven on us down ſhine;
Comforter, be Thy comfort mine!

Come, Father of the poor, to earth;
Come with Thy gifts of precious worth;
Come, Light of all of mortal birth!

Thou rich in comfort! Ever bleſt
The heart where Thou art conſtant gueſt,
Who giv'ſt the heavy-laden reſt.

Come, Thou in whom our toil is ſweet,
Our ſhadow in the noon-day heat,
Before whom mourning flieth fleet.

Bright Sun of Grace! Thy ſunſhine dart
On all who cry to Thee apart,
And fill with gladneſs every heart.

Whate'er without Thy aid is wrought,
Or ſkilful deed, or wiſeſt thought,
God counts it vain and merely nought.

O cleanſe us that we ſin no more,
O'er parched ſouls Thy waters pour;
Heal the ſad heart that acheth ſore.

Thy will be ours in all our ways;
Oh melt the frozen with Thy rays;
Call home the loſt in error's maze.

And grant us, Lord, who cry to Thee,
And hold the faith in unity,
Thy precious gifts of charity;

That we may live in holineſs,
And find in death our happineſs,
And dwell with Thee in laſting bliſs!

King Robert of France,
about A. D. 1000.

FIFTH SUNDAY AFTER EASTER.

These things have I spoken unto you, that in me ye might have peace. In the world ye shall have tribulation; but be of good cheer, I have overcome the world.—FROM THE GOSPEL.

CHRIST, Thou the champion of the band
who own
Thy cross, oh make Thy succour quickly
known;
The schemes of those who long our blood have sought
Bring Thou to nought.

Do Thou Thyself for us Thy children fight,
Withstand the devil, quell his rage and might,
Whate'er assails Thy members left below
Do Thou o'erthrow.

And give us peace; peace in the church and school,
Peace to the powers who o'er our country rule,
Peace to the conscience, peace within the heart,
Do Thou impart.

So shall Thy goodness here be still adored,
Thou guardian of Thy little flock, dear Lord,
And heaven and earth through all eternity
Shall worship Thee.

LOWENSTERN.

During the Thirty Years' War.

ASCENSION DAY.

This ſame Jeſus which is taken up from you into heaven, ſhall ſo come, in like manner as ye have ſeen him go into heaven.—FROM THE EPISTLE.

LORD, on earth I dwell in pain;
Here in anguiſh I muſt lie;
Wherefore leav'ſt Thou me again,
Why aſcendeſt Thou on high?
Take me, take me hence with Thee,
Or abide, Lord, ſtill in me;
Let Thy love and gifts be left,
That I be not all bereft.

Leave Thy heart with me behind,
Take mine hence with Thee away;
Let my ſighs an entrance find
To Thy heaven whene'er I pray.
When I cannot pray, oh plead
With Thy Father in my ſtead;
Thou who ſitt'ſt at God's right hand,
Help us here Thy faithful band.

Help me earthly toys to ſpurn,
Raiſe my thoughts from things below;
Mortal am I here, yet yearn
Heavenly like my Lord to grow,

That my time through faith may be
Order'd for eternity;
Till we riſe, all perils o'er,
Whither Thou haſt gone before.

In due ſeason come again,
As was promiſed us of old;
Raiſe the members that have lain
Gnaw'd of death beneath the mould.
Judge the evil world that deems
Thy ſure words but empty dreams;
Then for all our ſorrows paſt,
Let us know Thy joy at laſt.

NEUMANN. 1700.

SUNDAY AFTER ASCENSION DAY.

Theſe all confeſſed that they were ſtrangers and pilgrims on the earth. . . For they deſired a better country, that is, an heavenly; wherefore God is not aſhamed to be called their God: for He hath prepared for them a city.—HEB. xi. 13, 16.

HEAVENWARD doth our journey tend,
We are ſtrangers here on earth,
Through the wilderneſs we wend
Towards the Canaan of our birth.
Here we roam a pilgrim band,
Yonder is our native land.

Heavenward ſtretch, my ſoul, thy wings,
Heavenly nature canſt thou claim,
There is nought of earthly things
Worthy to be all thine aim;
Every ſoul whom God inſpires,
Back to Him its Source aſpires.

Heavenward! doth His Spirit cry,
When I hear Him in His Word,
Showing thus the reſt on high,
Where I ſhall be with my Lord:
When His Word fills all my thought,
Oft to heaven my ſoul is caught.

Heavenward ever would I haſte,
  When Thy Table, Lord, is ſpread;
Heavenly ſtrength on earth I taſte,
  Feeding on the Living Bread.
Such is e'en on earth our fare
Who Thy marriage feaſt ſhall ſhare.

Heavenwards! Faith diſcerns the prize
  That is waiting us afar,
And my heart would ſwiftly riſe,
  High o'er ſun and moon and ſtar,
To that Light behind the veil
Where all earthly ſplendours pale.

Heavenward Death ſhall lead at laſt,
  To the home where I would be,
All my ſorrows overpaſt,
  I ſhall triumph there with Thee,
Jeſus, who haſt gone before,
That we too might Heavenwards ſoar.

Heavenwards! Heavenwards! Only this
  Is my watchword on the earth;
For the love of heavenly bliſs
  Counting all things little worth.
Heavenward all my being tends,
Till in Heaven my journey ends.

SCHMOLCK. 1731.

WHIT-SUNDAY.

I will pray the Father, and He ſhall give you another Comforter, that He may abide with you for ever, even the Spirit of Truth.—FROM THE GOSPEL.

COME, deck our feaſt to-day
With flowers and wreaths of May,
And bring an offering pure and ſweet;
The Spirit of all grace
Makes earth His dwelling-place,
Prepare your hearts your Lord to meet;
Receive Him, and He ſhall outpour
Such light, all hearts with joy run o'er,
And ſound of tears is heard no more.

Thou harbinger of peace,
Who maketh ſorrows ceaſe,
Wiſdom in word and deed is Thine;
Strong hand of God, Thy ſeal
The loved of Jeſus feel;
Pure Light, o'er all our pathway ſhine!
Give vigorous life and healthy powers,
Oh let Thy ſevenfold gifts be ours,
Refreſh us with Thy gracious ſhowers!

Oh touch our tongues with flame,
When ſpeaking Jeſu's name!

And lead us up the heavenward road.
  Give us the power to pray,
  Teach us what words to ſay,
Whene'er we come before our God.
  O Higheſt Good, our ſpirits cheer,
  When raging foes are ſtrong and near,
  Give us brave hearts undimm'd by fear.

  O golden rain from heaven!
  Thy precious dews be given
Unto the churches' barren field!
  And let Thy waters flow,
  Where'er the ſowers ſow
The ſeed of truth, that it may yield
  A hundred-fold its living fruit,
  O'er all the land may take deep root,
  And mighty branches heavenward ſhoot.

  Thou fiery glow of Love!
  Let us Thy ardours prove,
Conſume our hearts with quenchleſs fire!
  Come, O Thou trackleſs Wind!
  Breathe gently o'er our mind!
Let not the fleſh to rule aſpire;
  Help us our free-born right to take,
  The heavy yoke of ſin to break,
  And all her tempting paths forſake.

  Be it Thine to ſtir our will;
  Our good intents fulfil;
Be with us when we go and come;
  Deep in our ſpirits dwell,
  And make their inmoſt cell

Thy temple pure, Thy holy home!
Teach us to know our Lord, that we
May call His Father ours through Thee,
Thou pledge of glories yet to be!

O make our crosses sweet,
And let Thy sunshine greet
Our straining eyes in clouded hours!
Wing Thou our upward flight
Toward yonder mountain bright,
Girded about with Zion's golden towers!
Forsake us not when our last foe
Puts forth his strength to lay us low,
Then, then our victory bestow!

Let us, while here we dwell,
This one thought ponder well,
That in God's likeness we are made.
As o'er a fruitful land
Rich harvests waving stand,
We, serving Him, bear fruits that never fade,
Till Thou in whom all comfort lies,
Lift us to fields above the skies,
And bid us bloom in Paradise!

Schmolck. 1715.

MONDAY IN WHITSUN-WEEK.

Would God that all the Lord's people were prophets, and that the Lord would put His Spirit upon them!—FROM THE LESSON.

COME to Thy temple here on earth,
Be Thou my ſpirit's gueſt,
Who giveſt us of mortal birth
A ſecond birth more bleſt;
Spirit beloved, Thou mighty Lord,
Who with the Father and the Son
Reigneſt upon an equal throne,
Art equally adored!

Oh enter, let me feel and know
Thy mighty power within,
That can alone our help beſtow,
And reſcue us from ſin.
Oh cleanſe my ſoul and make it white,
That I with heart unſtain'd and true,
May daily render ſervice due,
And honour Thee aright.

I was a wild unfruitful vine
Which Thou muſt prune and train;
Death pierced through all this life of mine,
But Thou my foe hath ſlain.

Thy holy baptiſm is his grave,
He periſhes beneath the flood
Of His moſt precious death and blood,
Who died our life to ſave.

Thou art the Spirit who doſt teach
To pray aright, for all
Our prayers are heard if Thou beſeech,
Thy ſongs have ſweeteſt fall.
They ſoar on tireleſs wings to heaven,
They fail not from before God's throne,
Till all His goodneſs we have known
By whom all help is given.

Thou art the Spirit of all joy,
Sadneſs Thou loveſt not;
Thy comfort beaming from on high,
Lights up the darkeſt lot,
Ah yes, how many a time of old
Thy voice hath wrapt my ſoul away,
To yon bright halls of endleſs day,
And oped the gates of gold!

Thou art the Spirit of all love,
Thou loveſt kindly life,
Wouldſt not that wrath our hearts ſhould move,
Nor envy, anger, ſtrife.
Thou hateſt hatred's withering reign,
In hearts that diſcord maketh dark
Doſt Thou rekindle love's bright ſpark,
And make them one again.

On Thee is all this world upſtaid,
And in Thy hands doth reſt;
Thou canſt the wayward heart perſuade
To turn as ſeems Thee beſt:
Oh therefore give Thy love and peace,
That they may join in ſtrongeſt bands
Long parted foes, and through our lands
Theſe ſad diviſions ceaſe.

Ariſe, and ſtem this tide of woe,
Of heartache, and of pain;
Call back Thy flock, and make them know
Bright days of joy again;
To peace and wealth the lands reſtore,
Waſted with fire or plague or ſword;
Come to Thy ruin'd churches, Lord,
And bid them bloom once more!

The rulers of our land defend,
Our Sovereign's throne uphold;
That he and we may proſper, ſend
True wiſdom to the old;
With piety the young men bleſs,
And through the nation ſhed abroad
True virtue and the fear of God,
A nation's happineſs.

Fill every heart with holy zeal
To keep the faith unſtain'd;
Let houſe and land Thy bleſſing feel,
Whence all true wealth is gain'd.

Him who resists Thy inward powers,
The Evil Spirit make Thou flee;
Whate'er delights Thy heart, would he
Fain root from out of ours.

Give strong and cheerful hearts to stand
Undaunted in the wars,
That Satan's works and mighty band
Are waging with Thy cause.
Help us to fight as warriors brave,
That we may conquer in the field,
And not one Christian man may yield
His soul to sin a slave.

Order according to Thy mind
Our life from day to day,
And when this life must be resign'd,
And Death has seized his prey,
When all our days have fleeted by,
Help us to die with fearless spirit,
And let us after death inherit
Eternal life on high.

PAUL GERHARDT.
During the Thirty Years' War.

TUESDAY IN WHITSUN-WEEK.

Hereby know ye the Spirit of God. Every ſpirit that confeſſeth that Jeſus Chriſt is come in the fleſh is of God.—From the Lesson.

COME, Holy Spirit, God and Lord,
Be all Thy graces now outpour'd
On the believer's mind and ſoul,
And touch their hearts with living coal.
Thy Light this day ſhone forth ſo clear,
All tongues and nations gather'd near,
To learn that faith, for which we bring
Glad praiſe to Thee, and loudly ſing,
Hallelujah, Hallelujah!

Thou Strong Defence, Thou Holy Light,
Teach us to know our God aright,
And call Him Father from the heart:
The Word of life and truth impart,
That we may love not doctrines ſtrange,
Nor e'er to other teachers range,
But Jeſus for our Maſter own,
And put our truſt in Him alone.
Hallelujah, Hallelujah!

Thou Sacred Ardour, Comfort Sweet,
Help us to wait with ready feet

And willing heart at Thy command,
Nor trial fright us from Thy band.
Lord, make us ready with Thy powers,
Strengthen the flesh in weaker hours,
That as good warriors we may force
Through life and death to Thee our course.
Hallelujah, Hallelujah!

LUTHER. 1524.

TRINITY SUNDAY.

And God ſaid, Let us make man in our image.—FROM THE LESSON.

MOST High and Holy Trinity!
Who of Thy mercy mild
Haſt form'd me here in Time, to be
Thy image and Thy child:
Oh let me love Thee day and night
With all my ſoul, with all my might;
Oh come, Thyſelf my ſoul prepare,
And make Thy dwelling ever there!

Father! repleniſh with Thy grace
This longing heart of mine,
Make it Thy quiet dwelling-place,
Thy ſacred inmoſt ſhrine!
Forgive that oft my ſpirit wears
Her time and ſtrength in trivial cares,
Enfold her in Thy changeleſs peace,
So ſhe from all but Thee may ceaſe!

O God the Son! Thy wiſdom's light
On my dark reaſon pour;
Forgive that things of ſenſe and ſight
Were all her joy of yore;

Henceforth let every thought and deed
On Thee be fix'd, from Thee proceed,
Draw me to Thee, for I would rise
Above these earthly vanities!

O Holy Ghost! Thou fire of love,
Enkindle with Thy flame my will;
Come with Thy strength, Lord, from above,
Help me Thy bidding to fulfil:
Forgive that I so oft have done
What I as sinful ought to shun;
Let me with pure and quenchless fire
Thy favour and Thyself desire!

Most High and Holy Trinity!
Draw me away far hence,
And fix upon eternity
All powers of soul and sense!
Make me at one within; at one
With Thee on earth; when life is done
Take me to dwell in light with Thee,
Most High and Holy Trinity!

ANGELUS. 1657.

FIRST SUNDAY AFTER TRINITY.

God is Love . . and herein is love, not that we loved God, but that He loved us.—FROM THE EPISTLE.

ON wings of faith, ye thoughts, fly hence,
Roam o'er Eternity's vast field,
Surpass the bounds of time and sense,
And rise to Him who hath reveal'd
That He is Love: there pause, and awestruck view
That ancient love with every morning new!

Ere earth's foundations yet were laid,
Or heaven's fair roof were spread abroad,
Ere man a living soul was made,
Love stirr'd within the heart of God;
Love fill'd the long futurity with good,
And grace to help at need beside her stood.

Thy loving counsel gave to me
True life in Christ Thy only Son,
Whom Thou hast made our way to Thee,
From whom all grace flows ever down.
Whose precious blood can make us pure and whole,
And bless and hallow all our inmost soul.

O Love, that long ere time began,
That precious name of child bestow'd;
That open'd Heaven on earth to man,
And call'd us sinners sons of God;
Thy gracious promptings move the Father's hand,
And on the page of life our names shall stand!

Ah happy hours, whene'er upſprings
My ſoul to yon Eternal Source,
Whence the glad river downward ſings,
Watering with goodneſs all my courſe,
So that each paſſing day anew I prove
How tender and how true my Father's love!

For what am I? At His command
The million creatures of His power
Start into life on ſea and land;
Oh why ſhould God ſuch bleſſings ſhower
On me, who am a leaf that fadeth faſt,
A little ſhifting duſt before the blaſt!

I am not worthy, Lord, that Thou
Shouldſt ſuch compaſſion on me ſhow;
That He who made the world ſhould bow
To cheer with love a wretch ſo low.
O Father, I would utterly reſign
Myſelf to Thee; take me, and make me Thine.

When ſtrength and heart grow faint and ſad,
From battling long with heavy pain,
Thy ſmile ſhines forth to make me glad,
Thou crowneſt me with joy again;
Then I behold Thy Spirit's wondrous power,
Whoſe work is mightieſt in our weakeſt hour.

Forth from Thy rich and bounteous ſtore
Life's common bleſſings daily flow,
More than we dare to aſk, far more
Than we deſerve, doſt Thou beſtow.
My heart diſſolves in tears of thankfulneſs,
To ſee how true Thy care, how quick to bleſs.

Nor here alone: hope pierces far
Through all the ſhades of earth and time;
Faith mounts beyond the fartheſt ſtar,
Yon ſhining heights ſhe fain would climb,
And gazing on eternity behold
The promiſed land, our heritage of old.

Can I with loveleſs heart receive
Tokens of love that never ceaſe?
Can I be thankleſs ſtill, and grieve
Him who is all my joy and peace?
Ah Friend of Man, were I to turn from Thee,
Myſelf were ſure my own worſt enemy.

Could I but honour Thee aright,
Noble and ſweet my ſong ſhould be;
That earth and heaven ſhould learn Thy might,
And what my God hath done for me.
There is no muſic ſweet as is Thy name,
No joy ſo deep as pondering o'er Thy fame.

O heart redeem'd! thou think'ſt it long
Till the appointed hour be come,
When thou ſhalt join the angels' ſong
To that Fair Love that brought thee home.
Have patience, heart; time hurries faſt away,
Soon ſhalt thou reach the one Eternal Day.

J. G. Hermann. 1747.

SECOND SUNDAY AFTER TRINITY.

And this is His commandment; That we ſhould believe on the name of His Son Jeſus Chriſt, and love one another, as He gave us commandment.—From the Epistle.

HEART and heart together bound,
Seek in God your true repoſe,
In your love the price be found
Of your Saviour's love and woes;
We the members, He the Head,
He the ſun, we beams He ſhowers,
Brethren by one Maſter led,
We are His, and He is ours.

Children of His realm draw near,
Make your covenant ſtronger ſtill,
From your hearts allegiance ſwear
Unto Him who conquer'd ill.
If your bonds are yet too weak,
If but fragile yet they prove,
Help from His good Spirit ſeek
Who can ſteel the chains of love.

Only ſuch love will ſuffice,
As the love that dwells in Him,
Love that from the croſs ne'er flies,
Love that ſpares not life or limb

'Twas for ſinners He was ſlain,
'Twas for foes He ſhed His blood,
That His death for all might gain
Endleſs life—the Higheſt Good.

Thus, O trueſt Friend, unite
All Thy conſecrated band,
That their hearts be ſet aright
To fulfil Thy laſt command.
Each muſt onward urge his friend,
Helping him in word and deed,
Love's bleſt pathway to aſcend,
Following where Thou, Lord, doſt lead.

Thou who doſt command that all
Practiſe love that bear Thy name,
Wake the dead, new followers call,
Touch the ſlothful with Thy flame.
Let us live, O Lord, at one,
As Thou with the Father art,
That through all the world be none
Of Thy members left apart.

Then were given what Thou haſt ſought,
In the Son were all men freed,
And the world at laſt were taught
That Thy rule is bleſt indeed.
Father of all ſouls, we praiſe
Thee who ſhineſt in the Son;
Lord, to Thee our hymns we raiſe,
Who haſt all men to Thee drawn!

After ZINZENDORF.
About 1731.

THIRD SUNDAY AFTER TRINITY.

Caſt all your care upon Him, for He careth for you.
—From the Epistle.

WHAT within me and without,
Hourly on my ſpirit weighs,
Burdening heart and ſoul with doubt,
Darkening all my weary days:
In it I behold Thy will,
God, who giveſt reſt and peace,
And my heart is calm and ſtill,
Waiting till Thou ſend releaſe.

God! Thou art my rock of ſtrength,
And my home is in Thine arms,
Thou wilt ſend me help at length,
And I feel no wild alarms.
Sin nor Death can pierce the ſhield
Thy defence has o'er me thrown,
Up to Thee myſelf I yield,
And my ſorrows are Thine own.

When my trials tarry long,
Unto Thee I look and wait,
Knowing none, though keen and ſtrong,
Can my truſt in Thee abate.

And this faith I long have nurſt,
  Comes alone, O God, from Thee;
Thou my heart didſt open firſt,
  Thou didſt ſet this hope in me.

Chriſtians! caſt on Him your load,
  To your tower of refuge fly;
Know He is the Living God,
  Ever to His creatures nigh.
Seek His ever-open door
  In your hours of utmoſt need;
All your hearts before Him pour,
  He will ſend you help with ſpeed.

But haſt thou ſome darling plan,
  Cleaving to the things of earth?
Leaneſt thou for aid on man?
  Thou wilt find him nothing worth.
Rather truſt the One alone
  Whoſe is endleſs power and love,
And the help He gives His own,
  Thou in very deed ſhalt prove.

On Thee, O my God, I reſt,
  Letting life float calmly on,
For I know the laſt is beſt,
  When the crown of joy is won.
In Thy might all things I bear,
  In Thy love find bitters ſweet,
And with all my grief and care
  Sit in patience at Thy feet.

O my ſoul, why art thou vex'd?
  Let things go e'en as they will;
Though to thee they ſeem perplex'd,
  Yet His order they fulfil.
Here He is thy ſtrength and guard,
  Power to harm thee here has none;
Yonder will He each reward
  For the works he here has done.

Let Thy mercy's wings be ſpread
  O'er me, keep me cloſe to Thee,
In the peace Thy love doth ſhed,
  Let me dwell eternally.
Be my All; in all I do
  Let me only ſeek Thy will,
Where the heart to Thee is true,
  All is peaceful, calm and ſtill.

A. H. Francke. 1663-1727.

FOURTH SUNDAY AFTER TRINITY.

I reckon that the ſufferings of this preſent time are not worthy to be compared with the glory that ſhall be revealed in us.—FROM THE EPISTLE.

WOULD'ST thou inherit life with Chriſt
on high?
Then count the coſt, and know
That here on earth below
Thou needs muſt ſuffer with thy Lord and die.
We reach that gain to which all elſe is loſs,
But through the croſs.

Oh think what ſorrows Chriſt Himſelf has known!
The ſcorn, and anguiſh ſore,
The bitter death He bore,
Ere he aſcended to His heavenly throne;
And deemeſt thou, thou canſt with right complain,
Whate'er thy pain?

Not e'en the ſharpeſt ſorrows we can feel,
Nor keeneſt pangs, we dare
With that great bliſs compare
When God His glory ſhall in us reveal,
That ſhall endure when our brief woes are o'er
For evermore!

SIMON DACH. 1640.

FIFTH SUNDAY AFTER TRINITY.

And who is he that will harm you, if ye be followers of that which is good? But and if ye suffer for righteousness' sake, happy are ye; and be not afraid of their terror, neither be troubled; but sanctify the Lord God in your hearts.—FROM THE EPISTLE.

IF God be on my side,
Then let who will oppose,
For oft ere now to Him I cried
And He hath quell'd my foes.
If Jesus be my Friend,
If God doth love me well,
What matters all my foes intend,
Though strong they be and fell.

Here I can firmly rest,
I dare to boast of this,
That God the Highest and the Best,
My Friend and Father is.
From dangerous snares He saves,
Where'er He bids me go
He checks the storms and calms the waves,
Nor lets aught work me woe.

I rest upon the ground
Of Jesus and His blood,
For 'tis through Him that I have found
The True Eternal Good.

Nought have I of mine own,
Nought in the life I lead,
What Christ hath given me, that alone
Is worth all love indeed.

His Spirit in me dwells,
O'er all my mind He reigns,
All care and sadness He dispels,
And soothes away all pains.
He prospers day by day
His work within my heart,
Till I have strength and faith to say,
Thou God my Father art!

When weakness on me lies
And tempts me to despair,
He speaketh words and utters sighs
Of more than mortal prayer;
But what no tongue can tell,
Thou God canst hear and see,
Who readest in the heart full well
If aught there pleaseth Thee.

He whispers in my breast
Sweet words of holy cheer,
How he who seeks in God his rest
Shall ever find Him near;
How God hath built above
A city fair and new,
Where eye and heart shall see and prove
What faith has counted true.

There is prepared on high
My heritage, my lot;
Though here on earth I fall and die,
My heaven ſhall fail me not.
Though here my days are dark,
And oft my tears muſt rain,
Whene'er my Saviour's light I mark,
All things grow bright again.

Who joins him to that Lord
Whom Satan flies and hates,
Shall find himſelf deſpiſed, abhorr'd,
For him the burden waits
Of mockery and ſhame,
Heap'd on his guiltleſs head;
And croſſes, trials, cruel blame,
Shall be his daily bread.

I knew it long ere now,
Yet am I not afraid;
The God to whom I pledged my vow,
Will ſurely ſend His aid.
At coſt of all I have,
At coſt of life and limb,
I cling to God who yet ſhall ſave,
I will not turn from Him.

The world may fail and flee,
Thou ſtandeſt faſt for ever,
Not fire, or ſword, or plague, from Thee
My truſting ſoul ſhall ſever.

No hunger, and no thirſt,
No poverty or pain,
Let mighty princes do their worſt,
Shall fright me back again.

No joys that angels know,
No throne or wide-ſpread fame,
No love or loſs, no fear or woe,
No grief of heart or ſhame—
Man cannot aught conceive
Of pleaſure or of harm,
That e'er could tempt my ſoul to leave
Her refuge in Thine arm.

My heart for gladneſs ſprings,
It cannot more be ſad,
For very joy it laughs and ſings,
Sees nought but ſunſhine glad.
The ſun that glads mine eyes
Is Chriſt the Lord I love,
I ſing for joy of that which lies
Stored up for us above.

PAUL GERHARDT. 1650.

SIXTH SUNDAY AFTER TRINITY.

Know ye not, that so many of us as were baptized into Christ, were baptized into His death?—FROM THE EPISTLE.

WELL for him who all things losing,
E'en himself doth count as nought,
Still the one thing needful choosing
That with all true bliss is fraught!

Well for him who nothing knoweth
But his God, whose boundless love
Makes the heart wherein it gloweth,
Calm and pure as saints above!

Well for him who all forsaking,
Walketh not in shadows vain,
But the path of peace is taking
Through this vale of tears and pain!

Oh that we our hearts might sever
From earth's tempting vanities,
Fixing them on Him for ever
In whom all our fulness lies!

Oh that we might Him discover
Whom with longing love we've sought,
Join ourselves to Him for ever,
For without Him all is nought!

Oh that ne'er our eyes might wander
  From our God, ſo might we ceaſe
Ever o'er our ſins to ponder,
  And our conſcience be at peace!

Thou abyſs of love and goodneſs,
  Draw us by Thy croſs to Thee,
That our ſenſes, ſoul and ſpirit,
  Ever one with Chriſt may be!

Anon.

SEVENTH SUNDAY AFTER TRINITY.

O Lord, how manifold are Thy works; in wisdom hast Thou made them all; the earth is full of Thy riches.—PSALM civ. 24.

GO forth, my heart, and seek delight
In all the gifts of God's great might,
These pleasant summer hours:
Look how the plains for thee and me
Have deck'd themselves most fair to see,
All bright and sweet with flowers.

The trees stand thick and dark with leaves,
And earth o'er all her dust now weaves
A robe of living green;
Nor silks of Solomon compare
With glories that the tulips wear,
Or lilies' spotless sheen.

The lark soars singing into space,
The dove forsakes her hiding-place,
And coos the woods among;
The richly-gifted nightingale,
Pours forth her voice o'er hill and dale,
And floods the fields with song.

Here with her brood the hen doth walk,
There builds and guards his nest the stork,
The fleet-wing'd swallows pass;

The ſwift ſtag leaves his rocky home,
And down the light deer bounding come
To taſte the long rich graſs.

The brooks ruſh gurgling through the ſand,
And from the trees on either hand,
Cool ſhadows o'er them fall;
The meadows at their ſide are glad
With herds; and hark! the ſhepherd lad
Sends forth his mirthful call.

And humming, hovering to and fro,
The never-wearied ſwarms forth go
To ſeek their honey'd food;
And through the vine's yet feeble ſhoots
Stream daily upwards from her roots
New ſtrength and juices good.

The corn ſprings up, a wealth untold,
A ſight to gladden young and old,
Who now their voices lift
To Him who gives ſuch plenteous ſtore,
And makes the cup of life run o'er
With many a noble gift.

Thy mighty working, mighty God,
Wakes all my powers; I look abroad
And can no longer reſt:
I too muſt ſing when all things ſing,
And from my heart the praiſes ring
The Higheſt loveth beſt.

I think, Art Thou ſo good to us,
And ſcattereſt joy and beauty thus
O'er this poor earth of ours;
What nobler glories ſhall be given
Hereafter in Thy ſhining heaven,
Set round with golden towers!

What thrilling joy when on our ſight
Chriſt's garden beams in cloudleſs light,
Where all the air is ſweet,
Still laden with the unwearied hymn
From all the thouſand ſeraphim
Who God's high praiſe repeat!

Oh were I there! Oh that I now,
Dear God, before Thy throne could bow,
And bear my heavenly palm!
Then like the angels would I raiſe
My voice, and ſing Thy endleſs praiſe
In many a ſweet-toned pſalm.

Nor can I now, O God, forbear,
Though ſtill this mortal yoke I wear,
To utter oft Thy name;
But ſtill my heart is bent to ſpeak
Thy praiſes; ſtill, though poor and weak,
Would I ſet forth Thy fame.

But help me; let Thy heavenly ſhowers
Revive and bleſs my fainting powers,
And let me thrive and grow

Beneath the ſummer of Thy grace,
And fruits of faith bud forth apace
While yet I dwell below.

And ſet me, Lord, in Paradiſe
When I have bloomed beneath theſe ſkies
Till my laſt leaf is flown;
Thus let me ſerve Thee here in time,
And after, in that happier clime,
And Thee, my God, alone!

PAUL GERHARDT. 1659.

EIGHTH SUNDAY AFTER TRINITY.

Brethren, we are debtors, not to the flesh, to live after the flesh. For if ye live after the flesh, ye shall die; but if ye through the Spirit do mortify the deeds of the body, ye shall live.—FROM THE EPISTLE.

O GOD, O Spirit, Light of all that live,
Who dost on us that sit in darkness shine,
Our darkness ever with Thy light doth strive,
In vain Thou lur'st us with Thy beams divine.
Yet none, O Spirit, from Thine eye can hide,
Gladly will I Thy searching glance abide.

Search all my hidden parts, whate'er impure
Thy Light discovers there, do Thou destroy;
The bitterest pain I willingly endure,
Such pain is follow'd by eternal joy.
Thou'lt cleanse me from my stains of darkest hue,
And in Christ's image form my soul anew.

I cannot stay the venom'd power of sin,
'Tis Thy anointing only can avail;
Oh make my spirit new and right within,
For without Thee my utmost efforts fail.
Life to my cold dead soul I cannot give,
Be Thou my life, so only shall I live.

O Breath from out the Eternal Silence, blow
All ſoftly o'er my ſpirit's barren ground,
All precious fulneſs of my God beſtow,
That where erſt ſin and ſhame alone were found,
Faith, love, and holy reverence may upſpring,
In ſpirit and in truth to worſhip God our King.

Oh let my thoughts, my actions and my will
Obedient ſolely to Thy impulſe move,
My heart and ſenſes keep Thou blameleſs ſtill,
Fix'd and abſorb'd in God's unutter'd love.
Thy praying, teaching, ſtriving, in my heart,
Let me not quench, nor make Thee to depart.

O Fount, O Spirit, who doſt take and ſhow
Things of the Son to us, who cryſtal clear,
From God's throne and the Lamb's, doſt ceaſeleſs
flow
Into the quiet hearts that ſeek Thee here;
I open wide my mouth, and thirſting ſink
Beſide Thy ſtream, its living waves to drink.

I give myſelf to Thee, to Thee alone,
From all elſe ſunder'd, Thou art ever near,
The creature and myſelf I all diſown,
Truſting with inmoſt faith that God is here!
O God, O Spirit, Light of Life, we ſee
None ever wait in vain, who wait for Thee.

TERSTEEGEN. 1731.

NINTH SUNDAY AFTER TRINITY.

How long halt ye between two opinions? If the Lord be God, follow Him; but if Baal, then follow him.—FROM THE LESSON.

WHY haltest thus, deluded heart,
Why waverest longer in thy choice?
Is it so hard to choose the part
Offer'd by Heaven's entreating voice?
Oh look with clearer eyes again,
Nor strive to enter in, in vain.
Press on!

Remember, 'tis not Cæsar's throne,
Nor earthly honour, wealth or might,
Whereby God's favour shall be shown
To him who conquers in this fight;
Himself and an eternity
Of bliss and rest He offers thee.
Press on!

God crowneth no divided heart;
Oh hallow to Him all thy life!
Who loveth Jesus but in part,
He works himself much pain and strife,
And gains what he deserveth well,
Here conflict, and hereafter hell.
Press on!

Who wreſtling long with many a cry,
 Can bid farewell at laſt to all;
Yet loveth ſtill the Lord moſt High,
 Loves Him alone whate'er befall,
Is counted worthy of the crown
And on a kingly throne ſet down.
 Preſs on!

Then break the rotten bonds away
 That hinder you your race to run,
That make you linger oft and ſtay;
 Oh be your courſe afreſh begun!
Let no falſe reſt your ſoul deceive,
Up! 'tis a Heaven ye muſt achieve!
 Preſs on!

Omnipotence is on your ſide,
 And wiſdom watches o'er your heads,
And God Himſelf will be your guide
 So ye but follow where He leads;
How many guided by His hand,
Have reach'd ere now their native land.
 Preſs on!

Let not the body dull the ſoul,
 Its weakneſs, fears, and ſloth deſpiſe;
Man toils and roams from pole to pole
 To gain ſome earthly fleeting prize,
The Higheſt Good he little cares
To win, or ſtriving ſoon deſpairs.
 Preſs on.

Oh help each other, haſten on,
  Behold the goal is nigh at hand;
Soon ſhall the battle-field be won,
  Soon ſhall your King before you ſtand!
To calmeſt reſt He leads you now,
And ſets His crown upon your brow.
Preſs on.

LEHR. 1733.

TENTH SUNDAY AFTER TRINITY.

As the hart panteth after the water brooks, even ſo panteth my ſoul after Thee, O God.—PSALM xlii. 1.

O GOD, I long Thy light to ſee,
My God, I hourly think on Thee;
Oh draw me up, nor hide Thy face,
But help me from Thy holy place.

Ah how ſhall I my freedom win?
How break this heavy yoke of ſin?
My fainting ſpirit thirſts for Thee,
Come, Lord, to help and ſet me free.

My heart is ſet to do Thy will,
But all my deeds are faulty ſtill;
My beſt attempts are nothing worth,
But ſoil'd with cleaving taint of earth.

Remember that I am Thy child,
Forgive whate'er my ſoul defiled,
Blot out my ſins, that I may riſe
Freely to Thee beyond the ſkies.

Help me to love the world no more,
Be Maſter of my houſe and ſtore,
The ſhield of faith around me throw,
And break the arrows of my foe.

Fain would my heart henceforward be
Fix'd, O my God, alone on Thee,
That heart and ſoul by Thee poſſeſt,
May find in Thee their perfect reſt.

Begone, ye pleaſures falſe and vain,
Untaſted, undeſired remain!
In heaven alone thoſe joys abound,
Where all my true delight is found.

Oh take away whate'er has ſtood
Between me and the Higheſt Good;
I aſk no better boon than this,
To find in God my only bliſs.

Anton Ulrich,
Duke of Brunſwick. 1667.

ELEVENTH SUNDAY AFTER TRINITY.

In Thy preſence is fulneſs of joy; at Thy right hand there are pleaſures for evermore.—PSALM xvi. 11.

O FRIEND of ſouls, how well is me
Whene'er Thy love my ſpirit calms!
From ſorrow's dungeon forth I flee,
And hide me in Thy ſhelt'ring arms.
The night of weeping flies away
Before the heart-reviving ray
Of love, that beams from out Thy breaſt;
Here is my heaven on earth begun;
Who were not joyful had he won
In Thee, O God, his joy and reſt!

The world may call herſelf my foe,
So be it; for I truſt her not,
E'en though a friendly face ſhe ſhow,
And heap with her good things my lot.
In Thee alone will I rejoice,
Thou art the Friend, Lord, of my choice,
For Thou art true when friendſhips fail;
'Mid ſtorms of woe Thy truth is ſtill
My anchor; hate me as it will,
The world ſhall o'er me ne'er prevail.

Through deſerts of the croſs Thou leadeſt,
I follow leaning on Thy hand;

From out the clouds Thy child Thou feedeſt,
And giv'ſt him water from the ſand.
I know Thy wondrous ways will end
In love and bleſſing, Thou true Friend,
Enough if Thou art ever near!
I know, whom Thou wilt glorify,
And raiſe o'er ſun and ſtars on high,
Thou lead'ſt through depths and darkneſs here.

To others Death ſeems dark and grim,
But not, Thou Life of life, to me;
I know Thou ne'er forſakeſt him
Whoſe heart and ſpirit reſt in Thee.
Oh who would fear his journey's cloſe,
If from dark woods and lurking foes,
He then find ſafety and releaſe?
Nay, rather with a joyful heart
From this dark region I depart,
To Thy eternal light and peace.

O Friend of ſouls, then well indeed
Is me, when on Thy love I lean!
The world, nor pain, nor death I heed,
Since Thou, my God, my joy haſt been.
Oh let this peace that Thou haſt given,
Be but a foretaſte of Thy heaven,
For goodneſs infinite is Thine.
Hence, world, with all thy flattering toys!
In God alone lie all my joys;
Oh rich delight, my Friend is mine!

DESZLER. 1692.

TWELFTH SUNDAY AFTER TRINITY.

Not that we are ſufficient of ourſelves to think anything as of ourſelves, but our ſufficiency is of God.—FROM THE EPISTLE.

WHO ſeeks in weakneſs an excuſe,
His ſins will vanquiſh never;
Unleſs he heart and mind renews,
He is deceived for ever.
The ſtraight and narrow way,
That ſhines to perfect day,
He hath not found, hath never trod;
Little he knows, I ween,
What prayer and conflict mean
To one who hath the light of God.

In what the world calls weakneſs lurks
The very ſtrength of evil,
Full mightily it helps the works
Of our great foe the devil.
Awake, my ſoul, awake,
Quickly thy refuge take
With Him, the Almighty, who can ſave:
One look from Chriſt thy Lord
Can ſever every cord
That binds thee now, a wretched ſlave.

Know, the firſt ſtep in Chriſtian lore
  Is to depart from ſin;
True faith will leave the world no more
  A place thy heart within.
    Thy Saviour's Spirit firſt
    The heavy bonds muſt burſt,
  Wherein Death bound thee in thy need;
    Then the freed ſpirit knows
    What ſtrength He gives to thoſe
  Who with their Lord are riſen indeed.

And what Thy Spirit, Lord, began
  Help Thou with inner might!
Earth has no better gift for man
  Than ſtrength and love of right.
    Oh make Thy followers juſt
    Who look to Thee in truſt,
  Thy ſtrength and juſtice let us know;
    Our ſouls through Thee would wear
    The power of grace, moſt fair
  Of all the jewels faith can ſhow.

Strong Son of God, break down Thy foes,
  So ſhall we conquer ours;
Strong in the might from Thee that flows,
  We mourn not lack of powers,
    E'er ſince that from above,
    The witneſs of Thy love
  Thy Spirit came, and doth abide
    With us, diſpelling fear
    And falſehood, that we here
  May fight and conquer on Thy ſide.

Give ſtrength, whene'er our ſtrength muſt fail;
  Give ſtrength the fleſh to curb;
Give ſtrength when craft and ſin prevail
  To weaken and diſturb.
    The world doth lay her ſnares
    To catch us unawares,
  Give ſtrength to ſweep them all away;
    So in our utmoſt need,
    And when death comes indeed,
  Thy ſtrength ſhall be our perfect ſtay.

MARPERGER. 1713.

THIRTEENTH SUNDAY AFTER TRINITY.

Then Hezekiah received the letter of the hands of the meſſengers, and read it, and Hezekiah went up into the houſe of the Lord, and ſpread it before the Lord.—From the Lesson.

LEAVE God to order all thy ways,
And hope in Him whate'er betide,
Thou'lt find Him in the evil days
Thy all-ſufficient ſtrength and guide;
Who truſts in God's unchanging love,
Builds on the rock that nought can move.

What can theſe anxious cares avail,
Theſe never-ceaſing moans and ſighs?
What can it help us to bewail
Each painful moment as it flies?
Our croſs and trials do but preſs
The heavier for our bitterneſs.

Only thy reſtleſs heart keep ſtill,
And wait in cheerful hope; content
To take whate'er His gracious will,
His all-diſcerning love hath ſent.
Doubt not our inmoſt wants are known
To Him who choſe us for His own.

He knows when joyful hours are beſt,
He ſends them as He ſees it meet;
When thou haſt borne the fiery teſt,
And art made free from all deceit,
He comes to thee all unaware,
And makes thee own His loving care.

Nor, in the heat of pain and ſtrife,
Think God hath caſt thee off unheard,
And that the man, whoſe proſperous life
Thou envieſt, is of Him preferr'd.
Time paſſes and much change doth bring,
And ſets a bound to everything.

All are alike before His face;
'Tis eaſy to our God moſt High
To make the rich man poor and baſe,
To give the poor man wealth and joy.
True wonders ſtill by Him are wrought,
Who ſetteth up, and brings to nought.

Sing, pray, and ſwerve not from His ways,
But do thine own part faithfully,
Truſt His rich promiſes of grace,
So ſhall they be fulfill'd in thee;
God never yet forſook at need
The ſoul that truſted Him indeed.

NEUMARCK. 1653.

FOURTEENTH SUNDAY AFTER TRINITY.

And they that are Chriſt's have crucified the fleſh with the affections and luſts.—FROM THE EPISTLE.

O CROSS, we hail thy bitter reign,
O come, thou well-beloved gueſt!
Whoſe soreſt ſufferings work not pain,
Whoſe heavieſt burden is but reſt.

Is not our Bleſſed Saviour bound
In cloſeſt ties of love to thoſe
Who faithful to the croſs are found,
Through ceaſeleſs tears, through ſaddeſt woes?

Hark, the confeſſors of the faith
Yet of their croſs and fetters boaſt;
All ſaints have borne it to the death,
With all the martyrs' radiant hoſt.

Pledge of our glorious home afar!
Thee, Holy Sign, with joy we take,
Sign of a peace life could not mar,
Of juſt content death could not ſhake.

Thou tell'ſt how Truth, once crucified,
Now throned in majeſty doth reign,

How love is bleſs'd and glorified,
  That here on earth was mock'd and ſlain.

Their names are writ in words of light
  Who before men their Lord confeſt;
The bridegroom's cry is heard at night,
  Come to my marriage feaſt, ye bleſt!

Who then would faint, nor joy to ſhare
  In Chriſt's reproach, in want or pain?
The bittereſt death who would not dare?
  Who fears a martyr's crown to gain?

Up, Brethren of the Croſs! and haſte
  Onward where Chriſt hath gone before!
We hymn His praiſe the while we taſte
  The ſhame and death He ſometime bore.

In bonds and ſtripes, in falſeſt blame,
  Our crown, our deareſt wealth we ſee,
A priſon were a throne, and ſhame
  Our chiefeſt glory, borne for Thee.

What though the world contempt may fling
  On us, though oft we ſtrive with death,
The holy angels ſpeed to bring
  Our help and ſtrength, our victor's wreath.

Up, quit the gates where ſin abides,
  From earth's doom'd cities quickly come,
Yon eaſtern Star full ſurely guides
  All pilgrims to their Father's home.

Gotter. 1697.

FIFTEENTH SUNDAY AFTER TRINITY.

Therefore take no thought, ſaying, What ſhall we eat, or what ſhall we drink . . for your Heavenly Father knoweth that ye have need of all theſe things. —From the Gospel.

BE thou content; be ſtill before
His face, at whoſe right hand doth reign
Fulneſs of joy for evermore,
Without whom all thy toil is vain.
He is thy living ſpring, thy ſun, whoſe rays
Make glad with life and light thy dreary days.
Be thou content.

Art thou all friendleſs and alone,
Haſt none in whom thou canſt confide?
God careth for thee, lonely one,
Comfort and help will He provide.
He ſees thy ſorrows and thy hidden grief,
He knoweth when to ſend thee quick relief;
Be thou content.

Thy heart's unſpoken pain He knows,
Thy ſecret ſighs He hears full well,
What to none elſe thou dar'ſt diſcloſe,
To Him thou mayſt with boldneſs tell.
He is not far away, but ever nigh,
And anſwereth willingly the poor man's cry.
Be thou content.

Why art thou full of anxious fear
How thou ſhalt be ſuſtain'd and fed?
He who hath made and placed thee here,
Will give thee needful daily bread.
Canſt thou not truſt His rich and bounteous hand,
Who feeds all living things on ſea and land?
Be thou content.

He who doth teach the little birds
To find their meat in field and wood,
Who gives the countleſs flocks and herds,
Each day their needful drink and food,
Thy hunger too will ſurely ſatisfy,
And all thy wants in His good time ſupply.
Be thou content.

Sayſt thou, I know not how or where,
No help I ſee where'er I turn;
When of all elſe we moſt deſpair,
The riches of God's love we learn;
When thou and I His hand no longer trace,
He leads us forth into a pleaſant place.
Be thou content.

Though long His promiſed aid delay,
At laſt it will be ſurely ſent;
Though thy heart ſink in ſore diſmay,
The trial for thy good is meant.
What we have won with pains we hold more faſt,
What tarrieth long is ſweeter at the laſt.
Be thou content.

Lay not to heart whate'er of ill
Thy foes may falſely ſpeak of thee,
Let man defame thee as he will,
God hears, and judges righteouſly.
Why ſhouldſt thou fear, if God be on thy ſide,
Man's cruel anger, or malicious pride?
Be thou content.

We know for us a reſt remains,
When God will give us ſweet releaſe
From earth and all our mortal chains,
And turn our ſufferings into peace.
Sooner or later death will ſurely come
To end our ſorrows, and to take us home.
Be thou content.

Home to the choſen ones, who here
Served their Lord faithfully and well,
Who died in peace, without a fear,
And there in peace for ever dwell.
The Everlaſting is their joy and ſtay,
The Eternal Word Himſelf to them doth ſay,
Be thou content.

PAUL GERHARDT. 1670.

SIXTEENTH SUNDAY AFTER TRINITY.

And when the Lord ſaw her, He had compaſſion on her and ſaid unto her, Weep not!—FROM THE GOSPEL.

LEAVE all to God,
Forſaken one, and ſtill thy tears.
For the Higheſt knows thy pain,
Sees thy ſufferings and thy fears;
Thou ſhalt not wait His help in vain,
Leave all to God.

Be ſtill and truſt!
For His ſtrokes are ſtrokes of love,
Thou muſt for thy profit bear;
He thy filial fear would move,
Truſt thy Father's loving care,
Be ſtill and truſt!

Know, God is near!
Though thou think Him far away,
Though His mercy long have ſlept,
He will come and not delay,
When His child enough hath wept,
For God is near!

O teach Him not
When and how to hear thy prayers;

Never doth our God forget,
He the croſs who longeſt bears
Finds his ſorrows' bounds are ſet,
Then teach Him not.

If thou love Him,
Walking truly in His ways,
Then no trouble, croſs or death,
Shakes thy heart, or quells thy praiſe.
All things ſerve thee here beneath,
If thou love God!

Anton Ulrich
Duke of Brunſwick. 1667.

SEVENTEENTH SUNDAY AFTER TRINITY.

I beſeech you that ye walk worthy of the vocation wherewith ye are called, with all lowlineſs and meekneſs, with longſuffering, forbearing one another in love; endeavouring to keep the unity of the ſpirit in the bond of peace.—FROM THE EPISTLE.

COME, brethren, let us go!
The evening cloſeth round,
'Tis perilous to linger here
On this wild deſert ground.
Take courage as ye wend
On towards eternity,
From ſtrength to ſtrength your courſe ſhall be,
And good at laſt your end.

We ſhall not rue our choice,
Though ſtrait our path and ſteep,
We know that He who call'd us here
His word ſhall ever keep.
Then follow, truſting; come,
And let each ſet his face
Toward yonder fair and bleſſed place,
Intent to reach our home.

The body and the houſe
Deck not, but deck the heart

With all your powers; we are but guefts,
Ere long we muft depart.
Eafe brings difeafe; content
Howe'er his lot may fall,
A pilgrim bears and bows to all,
For foon the time is fpent.

Come, children, let us go!
Our Father is our guide;
And when the way grows fteep and dark,
He journeys at our fide.
Our fpirits He would cheer,
The funfhine of His love
Revives and helps us as we rove,
Ah, bleft our lot e'en here!

Each haften bravely on,
Not yet our goal is near;
Look to the fiery pillar oft,
That tells the Lord is here.
Onward your glances fend,
Love beckons us, nor think
That they who following chance to fink,
Shall mifs their journey's end.

Come, children, let us go!
We travel hand in hand;
Each in his brother finds his joy
In this wild ftranger land.
As children let us be,
Nor by the way fall out,
The angels guard us round about,
And help us brotherly.

The ſtrong be quick to raiſe
The weaker when they fall;
Let love and peace and patience bloom
In ready help for all.
In love yet cloſer bound,
Each would be leaſt, yet ſtill
On love's fair path moſt pure from ill,
Moſt loving, would be found.

Come, wander on with joy,
For ſhorter grows the way,
Each riſing sun brings on the time
When in the grave we lay
The body down; awhile
Have truth and courage yet,
Your hopes above more fully ſet,
Careleſs of things more vile.

It will not laſt for long,
A little farther roam;
It will not laſt much longer now
Ere we ſhall reach our home;
There ſhall we ever reſt,
There with our Father dwell,
With all the ſaints who ſerved Him well,
There truly, deeply bleſt.

For this all things we dare,—
'Tis worth the riſk I trow,—
Renouncing all that clogs our courſe,
Or weighs us down below.

O world, thou art too ſmall,
We ſeek another higher,
Whither Chriſt guides us ever nigher,
Where God is all in all.

Friend of our perfect choice,
Thou Joy of all that live,
Being that know'ſt not chance or change,
What courage doſt Thou give!
All beauty, Lord, we ſee,
All bliſs and life and love,
In Him in whom we live and move,
And we are glad in Thee!

TERSTEEGEN. 1731.

EIGHTEENTH SUNDAY AFTER TRINITY.

Waiting for the coming of our Lord Jesus Christ, who shall also confirm you unto the end.—From the Epistle.

THOUGH all to Thee were faithless,
I yet were true my Head,
To show that love is deathless,
From earth not wholly fled.
Here didst Thou live in sadness,
And die in pain for me,
Wherefore I give with gladness,
My heart and soul to Thee.

I could weep night and morning
That Thou hast died, and yet
So few will heed Thy warning,
So many Thee forget.
O loving and true-hearted,
How much for us didst Thou!
Yet is Thy fame departed,
And none regards it now.

But still Thy love befriends us,
Of every heart the guide;
Unfailing help it lends us,
Though all had turn'd aside.

Oh! ſuch love ſoon or later
Muſt conquer, muſt be felt,
Then at Thy feet the traitor
In bitter tears ſhall melt.

Lord, I have inly found Thee,
Depart Thou not from me,
But wrap Thy love around me,
And keep me cloſe to Thee.
Once too my brethren, yonder
Upgazing where Thou art,
Shall learn Thy love with wonder,
And ſink upon Thy heart.

NOVALIS.

About 1795.

NINETEENTH SUNDAY AFTER TRINITY.

But ye have not ſo learned Chriſt; if ſo be that ye have heard Him, and have been taught by Him, as the truth is in Jeſus: that ye put off, concerning the former converſation, the old man, which is corrupt according to the deceitful luſts; and be renewed in the ſpirit of your mind; and that ye put on the new man, which after God is created in righteouſneſs and true holineſs.—FROM THE EPISTLE.

OH well for him who all things braves,
A ſoldier of the Lord to be,
Whom vice counts not among her ſlaves,
From envy, pride and paſſion free;
Who with the world of evil wars,
And bows his will beneath God's laws.

Who follows Chriſt whate'er betide,
Is worthy of a ſoldier's name;
Is He thy Way, thy Light, thy Guide,
'Tis meet thou alſo bear His ſhame:
Who ſhrinks from dark Gethſemane,
Shall Tabor's glories never ſee.

What profits it that Chriſt hath deign'd
To wear our mortal nature thus,
If we ourſelves have ne'er attain'd
That God reveal Himſelf in us?

The pure and virgin ſoul alone
He chooſeth for His earthly throne.

What profits it that Chriſt is born,
And bringeth childhood back to men,
Unleſs our long-loſt right we mourn,
And win through penitence again,
And lead a God-like life on earth,
As children of the ſecond birth?

What profits all that Chriſt hath taught,
If man is ſlave to reaſon ſtill,
And worldly wiſdom, honour, thought,
Rule all his acts, and move his will?
He follows what his Lord doth teach
Who true denial of ſelf would reach.

What profit us His deeds and life,
His meekneſs, love ſo quick to bleſs,
If we give place to pride and ſtrife,
Diſhonouring thus His holineſs?
What profits it, if for reward,
And not in faith, we call Him Lord?

What profits us His agony,
If we endure not pain and ſcorn?
'Tis combat brings forth victory,
Of ſorrow ſweeteſt joys are born;
And ne'er to him Chriſt's crown is given,
Who hath not here with Adam ſtriven.

What profit ye His death and croſs,
Unleſs to ſelf ye alſo die?

Ye love your life to find it loſs,
   Afraid the fleſh to crucify.
Wouldſt live to this world ſtill? Then know,
Chriſt's death to thee is barren ſhow.

What profit that he looſed and broke
   All bonds, if ye in league remain
With earth? Who weareth Satan's yoke
   Shall call Him Maſter but in vain.
Count ye the ſoul for reconciled,
Yet ſlave to earth, by ſin defiled?

What profits it that He is riſen,
   If dead in ſins thou yet doſt lie?
If yet thou cleaveſt to thy priſon,
   What profit that He dwells on high?
His triumph will avail thee nought,
If thou haſt ne'er the battle fought.

Then live and ſuffer, do and bear,
   As Chriſt thy pattern here hath done,
And ſeek His innocence to wear,
   That He may count thee of His own.
Who loveth Chriſt muſt live at war
With all that breaks His holy law.

Anon.

TWENTIETH SUNDAY AFTER TRINITY.

Singing and making melody in your heart unto the Lord; giving thanks always for all things unto God and the Father, in the name of our Lord Jeſus Chriſt. —FROM THE EPISTLE.

OH would I had a thouſand tongues,
To ſound Thy praiſe o'er land and ſea!
Oh! rich and ſweet ſhould be my ſongs,
Of all my God has done for me!
With thankfulneſs my heart muſt often ſwell,
But mortal lips Thy praiſes faintly tell.

Oh that my voice could far reſound
Up to yon ſtars that o'er me ſhine!
Would that my blood for joy might bound
Through every vein, while life is mine!
Would that each pulſe were gratitude, each breath
A ſong to Him who keeps me ſafe from death!

O all ye powers of ſoul and mind,
Ariſe, keep ſilence thus no more;
Put forth your ſtrength, and ye ſhall find
Your nobleſt work is to adore.
O ſoul and body, make ye pure and meet,
With heartfelt praiſe your God and Lord to greet.

Ye little leaves ſo freſh and green,
  That dance for joy in ſummer air,
Ye ſlender graſſes, bright and keen,
  Ye flowers ſo wondrous ſweet and fair;
Ye only live to ſhow your Maker's fame,
Help me his loving-kindneſs to proclaim.

O all ye living things that throng
  With breath and motion earth and ſky,
Be ye companions in my ſong,
  Help me to raiſe His praiſes high;
For my unaided powers are far too weak
The glories of His mighty works to ſpeak.

And firſt, O Father, praiſe to Thee
  For all I am and all I have,
It was Thy merciful decree
  That all thoſe bleſſings richly gave,
Which o'er the earth are ſcatter'd far and near,
To help and gladden us who ſojourn here.

And, deareſt Jeſus, bleſt be Thou,
  Whoſe heart with pity overflows,
Thou rich in help! who deign'dſt to bow
  To earth, and taſte her keeneſt woes;
Thy death has burſt my bonds and ſet me free,
Has made me Thine; henceforth I cling to Thee.

Nor leſs to Thee, O Holy Ghoſt,
  Be everlaſting honours paid,
For all Thy comfort, Lord, and moſt
  That I a child of life am made

By Thy deep lore; my good deeds are not mine,
Thou workest them through me, O light Divine.

Yes, Lord, through all my changing days,
With each new scene afresh I mark
How wondrously Thou guid'st my ways,
Where all seems troubled, wilder'd, dark;
When dangers thicken fast, and hopes depart,
Thy light beams comfort on my sinking heart.

Shall I not then be fill'd with joy,
Shall I not praise Thee evermore?
Triumphant songs my lips employ,
E'en when my cup of woe runs o'er.
Nay, though the heavens should vanish as a scroll,
Nothing shall shake or daunt my trusting soul.

But of Thy goodness will I sing
As long as I have life and breath,
Offerings of thanks I daily bring
Until my heart is still in death;
And when at last my lips grow pale and cold,
Yet in my sighs Thy praises shall be told.

Father, do Thou in mercy deign
To listen to my early lays;
Once shall I learn a nobler strain,
Where angels ever hymn Thy praise,
There in the radiant choir I too shall sing
Loud hallelujahs to my glorious King.

MENTZER. 1704.

TWENTY-FIRST SUNDAY AFTER TRINITY.

Be ſtrong in the Lord, and in the power of His might. Put on the whole armour of God, that ye may be able to ſtand againſt the wiles of the devil. For we wreſtle not againſt fleſh and blood, but againſt principalities, againſt powers, againſt the rulers of the darkneſs of this world, againſt ſpiritual wickedneſs in high places.—FROM THE EPISTLE.

GOD is our ſtronghold firm and ſure,
Our truſty ſhield and weapon,
He ſhall deliver us, whate'er
Of ill to us may happen.
Our ancient Enemy
In earneſt now is he,
Much craft and great might
Arm him for the fight,
On earth is not his fellow.

Our might is nought but weakneſs, ſoon
Should we the battle loſe,
But for us fights the rightful Man,
Whom God Himſelf doth chooſe.
Aſkeſt thou His name?
'Tis Jeſus Chriſt, the ſame
Whom Lord of Hoſts we call,
God only over all;
None from the field can drive Him.

What though the world were full of fiends,
  That would us sheer devour!
We know we yet shall win the day,
  We fear not all their power.
    The Prince of this world still
    May struggle as he will,
    He nothing can prevail,
    A word shall make him quail,
For he is judged of Heaven.

The word of God they shall not touch,
  Yet have no thanks therefor,
God by His Spirit and His gifts,
  Is with us in the war.
    Then let them take our life,
    Goods, honour, children, wife,
    Though nought of these we save,
    Small profit shall they have,
The kingdom ours abideth!

LUTHER. 1530.

TWENTY-SECOND SUNDAY AFTER TRINITY.

Truſt in the Lord with all thine heart, and lean not unto thine own underſtanding.—From the Lesson.

HOW bleſt to all Thy followers, Lord, the road
By which Thou lead'ſt them on, yet oft how ſtrange!
But Thou in all doſt ſeek our higheſt good,
For truth were true no longer, couldſt Thou change.
Though crooked ſeem the paths, yet are they ſtraight,
By which Thou draw'ſt Thy children up to Thee,
And paſſing wonders by the way they ſee,
And learn at laſt to own Thee wiſe and great.

No human laws can bind Thy Spirit, Lord,
That reaſon or opinion frame for us;
The knot of doubt is ſever'd by Thy ſword,
Or falls unravell'd if Thou willeſt thus.
The ſtrongeſt bonds are weak to Thee, O God,
All ſinks and fails that would Thy courſe oppoſe;
Thy lighteſt word can quell Thy ſtouteſt foes,
And deſert paths are by Thy footſteps trod.

What human prudence fondly ſtrives to bind,
Thy wiſdom ſunders far as eaſt from weſt;
We long beneath the yoke of man have pined,
Thy hand exalteth high above the reſt.
The world would ſcatter, Thou doſt union give;
She breaks, Thou buildeſt; what ſhe builds is made
A ruin'd heap; her light is nought but ſhade;
Her dead Thy Spirit calls to riſe and live.

Is there an act our reaſon would applaud?
Lo in Thy book haſt Thou the example given;
But him whom none as wiſe and pious laud,
Thou often lead'ſt in ſecret up to Heaven,
As Thou didſt leave the Phariſee, to go
And eat with ſinners whom all elſe forſook.
Who can ſearch out Thy purpoſes, or look
Into th' abyſs of wiſdom whence they flow?

Our all, O God, is nothing in Thine eyes,
Our nothing Thou regardeſt oft with love;
Glory and pomp of words Thou doſt not prize,
Thy impulſe only gives them power to move.
Thy nobleſt works awaken not man's praiſe,
For they are hidden, and he blindly turns
Away, nor though he ſee, their light diſcerns,
Too groſs his ſenſe, too keen their dazzling rays.

O Ruler! We would bleſs Thee and adore,
At whoſe command we live or turn to duſt;
When Thou doſt give us of Thy wiſdom's ſtore,
We ſee how true Thy care, and learn to truſt.

Thy wiſdom plays with us as with a child,
Who playing learns his Father loves him well;
'Tis love that brings Thee down with man to dwell,
Love guides our faltering footſteps through the wild.

Now ſeems to us o'er harſh and ſtrict Thy ſchool,
Now doſt Thou greet us mild and tenderly,
Now when our wilder paſſions break Thy rule,
Thy judgments fright us back again to Thee.
With downcaſt eyes we ſeek Thy face again,
Thou kiſſeſt us, we promiſe fair amends,
Once more Thy Spirit reſt and pardon ſends,
And curbs our paſſions with a ſtronger rein.

Thou know'ſt, O Father, all our weakneſs well,
Our impotence, our fooliſhneſs of mind;
Almoſt a paſſing glance may ſerve to tell
How weak are we, how ignorant, how blind.
Wherefore Thou comeſt with Thy help and ſtay,
A father's rule, a mother's love are Thine;
The lamb, on whom none elſe diſcern Thy ſign,
Thou carrieſt in Thy boſom day by day.

The common ways are trodden not of Thee,
Seldom Thy ſteps are traced by mortal eyes,
Yet art Thou near us, and unſeen, doſt ſee
All hopes and wiſhes that within us riſe.
The bright reflexion of Thy inner thought
Is day by day before our eyes outſpread;
Who thinks he quickeſt hath Thy meaning read,
Is oft another deeper leſſon taught.

O Eye, whoſe glance no falſehood can endure,
  Grant me to wiſely judge, and well diſcern,
Nature from grace—Thy Light ſerene and pure
  From groſſer fires that in and round me burn.
Let no ſtrange fire be kindled on the ſhrine
  Within my heart leſt I ſhould madly bring
  The hated offering unto Thee, O King.
Ah, bleſt the ſoul whoſe light is born of Thine!

When reaſon contradiĉts Thy law, or climbs
  So high, ſhe weeneth to know more than Thou,
Break down her confidence, great God, betimes,
  And teach her lowly at Thy feet to bow.
Nor let my proud heart diĉtate, Lord, to Thee,
  But tame the wayward will that ſeeks its own,
  And wake the love that clings to Thee alone,
And takes Thy judgments in humility.

Abſorb my will in Thine; ſupport and bear
  Onward in loving arms Thy timid child,
Thy Spirit's voice diſpels all doubt, all fear,
  And quells the paſſions erſt ſo fierce and wild.
Thou art mine, All, ſince that Thy Son is mine;
  Oh let Thy Spirit work with power in me,
  With ſtrong deſire I thirſt, I pant for Thee,
Oh joy whene'er Thy glories round me ſhhine!

So ſhall the creature ever ſerve me here,
  Nor angels bluſh to bear me company;
The perfeĉt ſplrits to Thy throne moſt near,
  They are my brethren, waiting there for me;

And oft my ſpirit joys to meet a heart,
That loveth Thee and me and every ſaint.
Is aught then left can make me ſad and faint?
Come, Fount of Joy! vain ſorrows, all depart!

GOTTFRIED ARNOLD. 1666-1714.

TWENTY-THIRD SUNDAY AFTER TRINITY.

For our converſation is in heaven ; from whence alſo we look for the Saviour, the Lord Jeſus Chriſt ; who ſhall change our vile body, that it may be faſhioned like unto His glorious body, according to the working whereby He is able even to ſubdue all things unto Himſelf.—From the Epistle.

LET who will in thee rejoice,
O thou fair and wondrous earth!
Ever anguiſh'd ſorrow's voice
Pierces through thy ſeeming mirth;
Let thy vain delights be given
Unto them who love not Heaven,
My deſire is fix'd on Thee,
Jeſus, deareſt far to me!

Weary ſouls with toil outworn,
Drooping 'neath the long hot light,
Wiſh that ſoon the coming morn
Might be quenched again in night,
That their toils might find a cloſe
In a ſoft and deep repoſe;
I but wiſh to reſt in Thee,
Jeſus, deareſt far to me!

Others dare the treacherous wave
Hidden rock and ſhifting wind,—

Storm and danger let them brave,
  Earthly good or wealth to find;
Faith ſhall wing my upward flight
Far above yon ſtarry height,
Till I find myſelf with Thee,
Jeſus, deareſt Friend to me!

Many a time ere now I ſaid,
  Many a time again ſhall ſay,
Would to God that I were dead,
  Would that in my grave I lay!
Reſt were mine, and ſweet my lot
Where the body hindereth not,
And the ſoul can ever be,
Jeſus, deareſt Lord, with Thee!

Come, O Death, thou twin of Sleep,
  Lead me hence, I pray thee come,
Looſe my rudder, through the deep
  Guide my veſſel ſafely home.
Thy approach who will may fly,
'Twere a joy to me to die,
For death opes the gates to Thee,
Jeſus, deareſt Friend to me!

Would that I to-day might leave
  This my earthly priſon here,
And my crown of joy receive
  Waiting me in yon bright ſphere!
In that home of joy, where dwell
Hoſts of angels, would I tell
How the Godhead ſhines in Thee,
Jeſus, deareſt Lord to me!

But not yet the gates of gold
  I may ſee nor enter in,
Nor the heavenly fields behold,
  But muſt ſit and mourning ſpin
Life's dark thread on earth below;
Let my thoughts then hourly go
Whither I myſelf would be,
Jeſus, deareſt Lord, with Thee!

J. Franck. 1653.

TWENTY-FOURTH SUNDAY AFTER TRINITY.

Jefus anfwered and faid unto her, Martha, Martha, thou art careful and troubled about many things: but one thing is needful, and Mary hath chofen that good part which fhall not be taken away from her.—LUKE x. 41, 42.

ONE thing is needful! Let me deem
Aright of that whereof He fpoke;
All elfe, how fweet foe'er it feem,
Is but in truth a heavy yoke,
'Neath which the toiling fpirit frets and pants,
Yet never finds the happinefs it wants:
This One can make amends whate'er I mifs,
Who hath it finds in all his joy through this!

My foul, wouldft thou this one thing find?
Seek not amid created things;
Leave what is earthly far behind,
O'er Nature heavenward ftretch thy wings,
Where God and man are One, in whom appear
All truth and fulnefs, thou haft found it here,—
The better part, the One thing needful He,
My One, my All, my Joy, who faveth me.

As Mary once devoutly fought
The Eternal truth, the better part,
And fat, enwrapt in holy thought,
At Jefu's feet with burning heart,

For nought elſe caring, yearning for the word
That ſhould be ſpoken by her Friend, her Lord,
Loſing her All in Him, His word believing,
And through the One all things again receiving:

Even ſo is all my heart's deſire
Fix'd, deareſt Lord, on Thee alone;
Oh make me true and draw me nigher,
And make Thyſelf, O Chriſt, my own.
Though many turn aſide to join the crowd,
To follow Thee in love my heart is vow'd,
Thy word is life and ſpirit, whither go?
What joy is there in Thee we cannot know?

All perfect wiſdom lies in Thee
As in its primal hidden ſource;
Oh let my will ſubmiſſive be,
And hold henceforth its even courſe,
Controll'd by truth and meekneſs, for high Heaven
To lowly ſimple hearts hath wiſdom given;
Who knoweth Chriſt aright, and in Him lives,
Hath won the higheſt prize that wiſdom gives.

Oh that my ſoul from ſleep might wake,
And ever, Lord, Thine image bear!
Thee for my portion I will take,
Thy holineſs Thou bidd'ſt us ſhare,
Whate'er we need for God-like walk and life
Is given to us in Thee; oh end this ſtrife,
And free me from the love of paſſing things,
To know alone the life from Thee that ſprings!

What can I ask for more? Behold
Thy mercy is a very flood;
I know that Thou hast pass'd of old
Into the Holiest through Thy blood,
And there redeem'd for ever those who lay
Beneath the rule of Satan; now are they
Made free by Thee, who erst were slaves and weak,
And childlike hearts the name of Father speak.

Deep joy and peace and holy calm
Fill my once restless spirit now;
O'er verdant pastures free from harm,
She follows Thee, her shepherd Thou;
Whate'er rejoices or consoles us here,
Is not so sweet as feeling Thou art near;
This One is needful, but all else is dross,
Let me win Christ, all other gain is loss.

SCHRODER. 1697.

TWENTY-FIFTH SUNDAY AFTER TRINITY.

Behold the days come, ſaith the Lord, that I will raiſe unto David a righteous Branch, and a King ſhall reign, and proſper, and ſhall execute judgment and juſtice in the earth.—FROM THE PASSAGE FOR THE EPISTLE.

REDEEMER of the nations, come!
Ranſom of earth, here make Thy home!
Bright Sun, oh dart Thy flame to earth,
For ſo ſhall God in Chriſt have birth!

Thou comeſt from Thy kingly throne,
O Son of God, the Virgin's Son!
Thou Hero of a two-fold race,
Walkeſt in might earth's darkeſt place.

Thou ſtoopeſt once to ſuffer here,
And riſeſt o'er the ſtarry ſphere;
Hell's gates at Thy deſcent were riven,
Thy aſcent is to higheſt Heaven.

One with the Father! Prince of might!
O'er nature's realm aſſert Thy right,
Our ſickly bodies pine to know
Thy heavenly ſtrength, Thy living glow.

How bright Thy lowly manger beams!
Down earth's dark vale its glory ſtreams,
The ſplendour of Thy natal night
Shines through all Time in deathleſs light.

J. FRANCK.
After St. Ambroſe.

ST. ANDREW'S DAY.

And Jesus saith unto them, Follow me. . . And they straightway left their nets, and followed Him.—From the Gospel.

FOLLOW me, in me ye live,
What ye ask I freely give,
Only heed ye lest ye stray,
Follow me the Living Way;
Follow me with all your hearts,
I will ward off sorrow's darts,
Learn from Christ your Lord to be
Rich in meek humility.

Yea, Lord, meet it is indeed
We should all Thy bidding heed;
Who in fear of this world's blame,
Counts Thy lowly yoke a shame,
To Thy name, Lord, hath no right,
Is no Christian in Thy sight.
Ah too well I know that we,
Here on earth, should follow Thee.

Where is strength, Lord, to fulfil,
Glad at heart, Thy works and will,
Following on where Thou hast trod?
All too weak am I, O God;

If awhile Thy paths I keep,
Soon I pine for reſt and ſleep;
E'en to love Thee, Lord, aright,
Paſſeth far my feeble might.

Yet I will not turn from Thee,
Yet my joy in Chriſt ſhall be;
Help me, make me ſtrong and bold,
Firm and faſt Thy grace to hold.
This world and her luſts I leave,
Only to my Lord I cleave;
All their promiſes are lies,
But who follows Thee is wiſe.

Thou haſt gone before us, Lord,
Not with anger, ſtrife, or ſword,
Not with kingly pomp and pride;
But with mercy at Thy ſide.
Moved by wondrous love divine
For our life Thou gaveſt Thine,
And Thy precious outpour'd blood,
Won for us the higheſt good.

Let us follow in ſuch ſort,
Chriſt-like every deed and thought,
That Thy love moſt true and kind
Henceforth all our hearts may bind;
None may look behind him now,
Who to Chriſt hath pledged his vow;
Chriſt doth lead, no longer ſtand,
Follow me, is His command.

Draw me up, my God, from hence,
Raiſe me high o'er earth and ſenſe,
That I loſe not Thee from ſight,
Nor in life nor death, my Light!
In my ſoul's moſt deep receſs
Let me cheriſh holineſs,
Not for ſhow or human praiſe,
But for Thy ſake, all my days.

Grant me, Lord, my heart's deſire,
So my courſe to run nor tire,
That my practiſed ſoul may prove
What Thy meekneſs, what Thy love.
Grant me here to truſt Thy grace,
There with joy to ſee Thy face,
This in time my portion be,
That through all eternity!

Rist. 1644.

ST. THOMAS THE APOSTLE.

And Thomas anſwered and ſaid unto Him, My Lord and my God. Jeſus ſaith unto him, Thomas, because thou haſt ſeen me thou haſt believed; bleſſed are they that have not ſeen, and yet have believed.—FROM THE GOSPEL.

LONG in the ſpirit-world my ſoul had ſought
Some friendly being, cloſe to her akin;
Long had prepared a dwelling in her thought
And heart for ſuch an one; for ſhe could win
Through Him alone her ſtrength, for Him ſhe yearn'd,
Toward Him her fervent longing ever burn'd.

And rich the world in things inviſible,
In heathen gods, and ſpirits great and ſmall,
And bright and dark; yet ever did ſhe dwell
Alone, for One was wanting 'mid them all;
One having might and glory, rich in love,
God, who as man could ſhame and weakneſs prove.

Then came the Word, and took on Him our fleſh,
And dwelt with men, here in the world of ſight,
And made an end of ſtrife, and link'd afreſh
Our ſinful earth unto the throne of light.
Into His ancient glory He is gone,
And yet He dwells with us till time be done.

Thus, O my ſoul, haſt thou received thy will;
  The glory of the world of ghoſts is dim
Before the One, who is, and was, and ſtill
  Shall ever be; all hearts are ſix'd on Him,
And ſpirit worlds, ſince He is there, become
Hallow'd and ſafe to thee, thy proper home.

Thou ſoareſt now through all their heights ſublime,
  And not as once doth empty back return,
But gazing on thy God, forgetteſt time
  Beneath His loving glance, whence thou wouldſt
      learn
How thou ſhouldſt love, and know His Word aright:
Ah bleſt the love and faith that aſk not ſight!

ALBERTINI. 1821.

PRESENTATION IN THE TEMPLE.

Lord, now lettest Thou Thy servant depart in peace, according to Thy word; for mine eyes have seen Thy salvation.—From the Gospel.

LIGHT of the Gentile world!
Thy people's joy and love!
Drawn by Thy Spirit we are come
Thy presence, Lord, to prove.
Within Thy temple walls
We wait with earnest mind,
As Simeon waited long of old
His Saviour God to find.

Thou wilt be found of us,
O Lord, in every place,
Where Thou hast promised faithfully
We should behold Thy face.
Thou yet dost suffer us
Who oft are gather'd here,
To bear Thee in the arms of faith
As once that aged seer.

Be Thou our bliss, our light,
Shining 'mid pain and loss,
Our Sun of strength in time of fear,
The glory round our cross;

A glow in ſinking hearts,
A ſunbeam in diſtreſs,
Phyſician, nurſe, in ſickneſs' hours,
In death our happineſs!

Oh let us, Lord, prevail
With Simeon at the laſt;
May we take up his dying ſong
When life is waning faſt!
"Let me depart in peace,
Since that mine aged eyes
Have ſeen the Saviour here on earth,
Have ſeen His glory riſe."

Yes, with the eye of faith
My Jeſus I behold;
No foe can rob me of my Lord,
Though fierce his threats and bold.
I dwell within Thy heart,
Thou doſt in mine abide,
Not ſorrow, pain nor death itſelf,
Can tear me from Thy ſide.

J. Franck. 1653

ST. MATTHIAS' DAY.

Come unto me, all ye that labour and are heavy aden, and I will give you reſt.—FROM THE GOSPEL.

YES, there remaineth yet a reſt!
Ariſe, ſad heart, that darkly pines,
By heavy care and pain oppreſt,
On whom no ſun of gladneſs ſhines;
Look to the Lamb! in yon bright fields
Thou'lt know the joy His preſence yields;
Caſt off thy load and thither haſte;
Soon ſhalt thou fight and bleed no more,
Soon, ſoon thy weary courſe be o'er,
And deep the reſt thou then ſhalt taſte.

The reſt appointed thee of God,
The reſt that nought ſhall break or move,
That ere this earth by man was trod
Was ſet apart for thee by Love.
Our Saviour gave His life to win
This reſt for thee; oh enter in!
Hear how His voice ſounds far and wide,
Ye weary ſouls, no more delay,
Loiter not faithleſs by the way,
Here in my peace and reſt abide!

Ye heavy-laden, come to Him!
Ye who are bent with many a load,
Come from your priſons drear and dim,
Toil not thus ſadly of your road!

Ye've borne the burden of the day,
And hear ye not your Saviour ſay,
I am your refuge and your reſt?
His children ye, of heavenly birth,
Howe'er may rage ſin, hell, or earth,
Here are ye ſafe, here calmly bleſt.

Yonder in joy the ſheaves we bring,
Whoſe ſeed was ſown on earth in tears;
There in our Father's houſe we ſing
The ſong too ſweet for mortal ears.
Sorrow and ſighing all are paſt,
And pain and death are fled at laſt,
There with the Lamb of God we dwell,
He leads us to the cryſtal river,
He wipes away all tears for ever;
What there is ours no tongue can tell.

Hunger nor thirſt can pain us there,
The time of recompenſe is come,
Nor cold nor ſcorching heat we bear,
Safe ſhelter'd in our Saviour's home.
The Lamb is in the midſt; and thoſe
Who follow'd Him through ſhame and woes,
Are crown'd with honour, joy and peace.
The dry bones gather life again,
One Sabbath over all ſhall reign,
Wherein all toil and labour ceaſe.

There is untroubled calm and light,
No gnawing care ſhall mar our reſt;
Ye weary, heed this word aright,
Come, lean upon your Saviour's breaſt.

Fain would I linger here no more,
Fain to yon happier world upſoar,
  And join that bright expectant band.
    Oh raiſe, my ſoul, the joyful ſong
    That rings through yon triumphant throng;
  Thy perfect reſt is nigh at hand.

KUNTH. 1733.

THE ANNUNCIATION.

Behold the handmaid of the Lord; be it unto me according to Thy word.—FROM THE GOSPEL.

YEA, my ſpirit fain would ſink
In Thy heart and hands, my God,
Waiting till Thou ſhow the end
Of the ways that Thou haſt trod;
Stripp'd of ſelf, how calm her reſt
On her loving Father's breaſt!

And my ſoul repineth not,
Well content whate'er befall;
Murmurs, wiſhes, of ſelf-will,
They are ſlain and vanquiſh'd all,
Reſtleſs thoughts, that fret and crave,
Slumber in her Saviour's grave.

And mv ſoul is free from care,
For her thoughts from all things ceaſe
That can pierce like ſharpeſt thorns,
Wounding ſore the inner peace.
He who made her careth well,
She but ſeeks in peace to dwell.

And my ſoul deſpaireth not,
Loving God amid her woe;
Grief that wrings and breaks the heart
Only they who hate Him know:

They who love Him ſtill poſſeſs
Comfort in their worſt diſtreſs.

And my ſoul complaineth not,
  For ſhe knows not pain or fear,
Clinging to her God in faith,
  Truſting though He ſlay her here
'Tis when fleſh and blood repine,
Sun of joy, Thou canſt not ſhine.

Thus my ſoul before her God
  Lieth ſtill, nor ſpeaketh more,
Conqueror thus o'er pain and wrong,
  That once ſmote her to the core;
Like a ſilent ocean, bright
With her God's great praiſe and light.

WINKLER. 1713.

ST. BARNABAS' DAY.

We preach unto you that ye ſhould turn from theſe vanities unto the living God which made heaven, and earth, and the ſea, and all things that are therein: who in time paſt ſuffered all nations to walk in their own ways. Nevertheleſs He left not Himſelf without witneſs, in that He did good, and gave us rain from heaven, and fruitful ſeaſons, filling our hearts with food and gladneſs.—FROM THE LESSON.

SHALL I not ſing praiſe to Thee,
Shall I not give thanks, O Lord?
Since in every thing I ſee
How Thy love keeps watch and ward
O'er us, how the trueſt love
Ever fills Thy heart, my God,
Bearing, cheering, on their road,
All who in Thy ſervice move.
All things elſe have but their day,
God's love only laſts for aye.

As the eagle o'er her neſt
Spreads her ſheltering wings abroad,
So from all that would moleſt,
Doth Thine arm defend me, Lord;
From my youth up e'en till now,
Of the being Thou didſt give,

And the life that ſtill I live,
Faithful Guardian ſtill wert Thou.
All things elſe have but their day,
God's love only laſts for aye.

Nay He kept not back His Son,
But hath given Him for our good,
And our ſafety He hath won
By the ſhedding of His blood.
O Thou fathomleſs abyſs!
My weak powers but ſtrive in vain,
Knowledge of Thy depths to gain,
Man knows not ſuch love as this.
All things elſe have but their day,
God's love only laſts for aye.

And His Spirit, bleſſed Guide,
In His holy Word doth teach,
How on earth we may abide,
So that heaven at laſt we reach;
Every longing heart doth fill
With the pure true light of faith,
That can break the bonds of death,
And control the powers of ill.
All things elſe have but their day,
God's love only laſts for aye.

Truly hath he cared indeed
For my ſoul's health, and no leſs
If my body ſuffer need,
Will He help in my diſtreſs.
When my ſtrength and courage fail,
When my powers can do no more,

Doth my God ſuch ſtrength outpour,
That I riſe up and prevail.
All things elſe have but their day,
God's love only laſts for aye.

All the hoſts of heaven and earth,
Hath He placed at my command,
Nowhere is there lack or dearth,
But I find in ſea and land
All things order'd for my wants,
Living things in fields and woods,
On the heights or in the floods,
And the earth brings forth her plants.
All things elſe have but their day,
God's love only laſts for aye.

When I ſleep my Guardian wakes,
And revives my wearied mind;
Every morning on me breaks
With ſome mark of love moſt kind;
Had my God not ſtood my Friend,
Had His countenance not been
Here my guide, I had not ſeen
Many a trial reach its end.
All things elſe have but their day,
God's love only laſts for aye.

Often hath my crafty Foe
Threaten'd to bring down on me
Many a ſore and heavy woe,
From which yet my life is free;
For the angel whom God ſends,
Wards off every threaten'd hurt,

Every evil doth avert
That mine Enemy intends.
All things elſe have but their day,
God's love only laſts for aye.

As a father ne'er withdraws
From a child His all of love,
Though it often break his laws,
Though it careleſs, wilful, prove:
Even ſo my loving Lord
Doth my faults with pity ſee,
With His rod He chaſteneth me,
Not avenging with His ſword.
All things elſe have but their day,
God's love only laſts for aye.

When His ſtrokes upon me light,
Bitterly I feel their ſmart,
Yet are they, if ſeen aright,
Tokens that my Father's heart
Yearns to bring me back again
Through theſe croſſes to His fold,
From the world that fain would hold
Soul and body in its chain.
All things elſe have but their day,
God's love only laſts for aye.

All my life I ſtill have found,
And I will forget it never,
Every ſorrow hath its bound,
And no croſs endures for ever.
After all the winter's ſnows
Comes ſweet ſummer back again,

Patient souls ne'er wait in vain,
Joy is given for all their woes.
All things else have but their day,
God's love only lasts for aye.

Since then neither change nor end,
In Thy love can e'er have place,
Father! I beseech Thee send
Unto me Thy loving grace.
Help Thy feeble child, and give
Strength to serve Thee day and night,
Loving Thee with all my might,
While on earth I yet must live;
So shall I when Time is o'er,
Praise and love Thee evermore.

PAUL GERHARDT. 1659.

ST. MICHAEL AND ALL ANGELS.

Are they not all miniſtering ſpirits, ſent forth to miniſter for them that ſhall be heirs of ſalvation?—HEB. i. 14.

PRAISE and thanks to Thee be ſung,
Mighty God, in ſweeteſt tone!
Lo! from every land and tongue,
Nations gather round Thy throne,
Praiſing Thee, that Thou doſt ſend,
Daily from Thy Heaven above,
Angel-meſſengers of love,
Who Thy threaten'd Church defend.
Who can offer worthily,
Lord of angels, praiſe to Thee!

'Tis your office, Spirits bright,
Still to guard us night and day,
And before your heavenly might,
Powers of darkneſs flee away;
Ever doth your unſeen hoſt,
Camp around us, and avert
All that ſeek to do us hurt,
Curbing Satan's malice moſt.
Lord, who then can worthily,
For ſuch goodneſs honour Thee!

And ye come on ready wing,
When we drift toward ſheer deſpair,
Seeing nought where we might cling,
Suddenly, lo, ye are there!

And the wearied heart grows ſtrong,
As an angel ſtrengthen'd Him,
Fainting in the garden dim,
'Neath the world's vaſt woe and wrong.
Lord, who then can worthily,
For ſuch mercy honour Thee!

Right and ſeemly were it then
We ſhould glory that our God
Hath ſuch honour put on men,
That He ſends o'er earth abroad
Princes of the realm above,
Champions, who by day and night,
Shield us with His holy might;
Come, behold how great His love!
Lord, who then can worthily,
For ſuch favour honour Thee!

Praiſe and thanks to Thee be ſung,
Mighty God, in ſweeteſt tone.
Lo! from every land and tongue,
Nations gather round Thy throne,
Praiſing Thee, that Thou doſt ſend,
Hourly from Thy glorious ſphere,
Angels down to help us here,
And Thy threaten'd Church defend.
Let us henceforth worthily,
Lord of angels, honour Thee.

Rist. 1655.

ALL SAINTS' DAY.

Lo, a great multitude which no man could number, of all nations, and kindreds, and people, and tongues, ſtood before the throne and before the Lamb, clothed with white robes, and palms in their hands; and cried with a loud voice, ſaying, Salvation to our God which ſitteth upon the throne and unto the Lamb.—FROM THE EPISTLE.

WHO are thoſe before God's throne,
What the crowned hoſt I ſee?
As the ſky with ſtars thick-ſtrown
Is their ſhining company:
Hallelujahs, hark, they ſing,
Solemn praiſe to God they bring.

Who are thoſe that in their hands
Bear aloft the conqueror's palm,
As one o'er his foeman ſtands,
Fallen beneath his mighty arm?
What the war and what the ſtrife,
Whence came ſuch victorious life?

Who are thoſe array'd in light,
Cloth'd in righteouſneſs divine,
Wearing robes moſt pure and white,
That unſtain'd ſhall ever ſhine,
That can nevermore decay;
Whence came all this bright array?

They are thoſe who, ſtrong in faith,
  Battled for the mighty God;
Conquerors o'er the world and death,
  Following not Sin's crowded road;
Through the Lamb who once was ſlain,
Did they ſuch high victory gain.

They are thoſe who much have borne,
  Trial, ſorrow, pain, and care,
Who have wreſtled night and morn
  With the mighty God in prayer;
Now their ſtrife hath found its cloſe,
God hath turn'd away their woes.

They are branches of that Stem,
  Who hath our Salvation been,
In the blood He ſhed for them,
  Have they made their raiment clean;
Hence they wear ſuch radiant dreſs,
Clad in ſpotleſs holineſs.

They are thoſe who hourly here
  Served as prieſts before their Lord,
Offering up with gladſome cheer
  Soul and body at His word.
Now within the Holy Place,
They behold Him face to face.

As the harts at noonday pant
  For the river freſh and clear,
Did their ſouls oft long and faint,
  For the Living Fountain here.

Now their thirſt is quench'd, they dwell
With the Lord they loved ſo well.

Thitherwards I ſtretch my hands,
O Lord Jeſus; day by day,
In Thy houſe in theſe ſtrange lands,
Compaſs'd round with foes, I pray,
Let me ſink not in the war,
Drive for me my foes afar.

Caſt my lot in earth and heaven
With Thy ſaints made like to Thee,
Let my bonds be alſo riven,
Make Thy child who loves Thee free;
Near the throne where Thou doſt ſhine,
May a place at laſt be mine.

Ah! that bliſs can ne'er be told,
When with all that army bright,
Thee, my Sun, I ſhall behold,
Shining ſtar-like with Thy light.
Amen! Thanks be brought to Thee,
Praiſe through all eternity.

SCHENK. Died 1727.

MORNING HYMNS.

MORNING HYMNS.

I.

GOD who madeſt earth and heaven,
Father, Son, and Holy Ghoſt,
Who the day and night haſt given,
Sun and moon and ſtarry hoſt,
Thou whoſe mighty hand maintains
Earth and all that ſhe contains;

God, I thank Thee from my heart,
That through all the livelong night,
Thou haſt kept me ſafe apart
From all danger, pain, affright,
And the cunning of my foe,
Hath not wrought my overthrow.

Let the night of ſin depart,
As this earthly night hath fled;
Jeſus, take me to Thy heart,
In the blood that Thou haſt ſhed
Is my help and hope alone,
For the evil I have done.

Help me as each morn ſhall break,
In the ſpirit to ariſe,
Let my ſoul from ſin awake,
That when o'er the aged ſkies,
Thy great Judgment Day appear,
I may ſee it free from fear.

Ever lead me, ever guide
  All my wanderings by Thy Word;
As Thou haſt been, ſtill abide
  My defence, my refuge, Lord.
Never ſafe except with Thee,
Ever Thou my Guardian be!

Mighty God, I now commend
  Soul and body unto Thee,
All the powers that Thou doſt lend,
  By Thy hand directed be;
Thou my boaſt, my ſtrength divine,
Keep me with Thee, I am Thine.

Let Thine angel guard my ſoul
  From the Evil One's dark power,
All his thouſand wiles control,
  Warning, guiding me each hour,
Till my final reſt be come,
And Thine angel bear me home.

HEINRICH ALBERT. 1644.

II.

THE golden ſunbeams with their joyous gleams,
  Are kindling o'er earth, her life and mirth,
Shedding forth lovely and heart-cheering light;
  Through the dark hours' chill I lay ſilent and ſtill,
  But riſen at length to gladneſs and ſtrength,
I gaze on the heavens all glowing and bright.

Mine eyes now behold Thy works, that of old
And ever are telling to all men here dwelling,
How great is Thy glory, how wondrous Thy power;
They tell of the home where the faithful ſhall come,
Who depart to that peace that can change not or
ceaſe,
From earth where all paſſeth as paſſes the hour.

Come let us raiſe our voices, and praiſe
The Maker of all, at His feet let us fall,
Offering to Him again all He hath given;
The beſt that is ours, our hearts and our powers,
Glad ſongs that we ſing Him, thanks that we
bring Him—
Theſe are the incenſe moſt grateful to Heaven.

Evening and morning thus ever He cares for us,
Bleſſing, renewing, warding off ruin,
Theſe are His works, thus His goodneſs we prove;
When we are ſleeping, watch He is keeping,
When we ariſe, He gladdens our eyes
With the ſunſhine of mercy, the glow of His love.

All paſſeth away, but God liveth aye,
And changeth in nought; eternal His Thought,
His Word and His Will are ſteadfaſt and ſure;
Never His grace nor His mercy decays,
It heals the ſad heart from its deadlieſt ſmart,
Giving it life that ſhall ever endure.

God, Thou my crown! forgiving look down,
And hide from Thy face through Thy pitying
grace,

All my tranſgreſſions againſt Thy command;
Henceforth oh rule me, guide me and ſchool me,
As Thou ſeeſt fit; my ways I commit
All to Thy pleaſure, Thy merciful hand.

Croſſes and ſorrow may end with the morrow,
Stormieſt ſeas ſhall ſink into peace,
The wild winds are huſh'd, and the ſunſhine returns;
So fulneſs of reſt, and the calm of the bleſt,
Are waiting me there, in that garden moſt fair,
That home for which daily my ſpirit here yearns.

PAUL GERHARDT.

III.

COME, my ſoul, awake, 'tis morning,
Day is dawning
O'er the earth, ariſe and pray;
Come, to Him who made this ſplendour,
Thou muſt render
All thy feeble powers can pay.

From the ſtars now learn thy duty,
See their beauty
Paling in the golden air;
So God's light Thy miſts ſhould baniſh,
Thus ſhould vaniſh
What to darken'd ſenſe ſeem'd fair.

See how everything that liveth,
Gladly ſtriveth
On the pleaſant light to gaze;
Stirs with joy each thing that groweth,
As it knoweth
Darkneſs ſmitten by its rays.

Soul, thy incenſe alſo proffer;
Thou ſhouldſt offer
Praiſe to Him, who from thy head
Kept afar the ſtorms of ſorrow,
That the morrow
Finds the night in peace hath fled.

Bid Him bleſs what thou art doing,
If purſuing
Some good aim; but if there lurks
Ill intent in thine endeavour,
May He ever
Thwart and turn thee from thy works.

Think that He, the All-diſcerning,
Knows each turning
Of thy path, each ſinful ſtain;
Nay what ſhame would fain gloſs over,
Can diſcover;
All thou doſt to Him is plain.

Bound unto the flying hours
Are our powers;
Earth's vain good floats down their wave,
That thy ſhip, my ſoul, is haſting,
Never reſting,
To its haven in the grave.

Pray that when thy life is closing,
Calm reposing,
Thou mayst die, and not in pain;
That the night of death departed,
Thou glad-hearted,
Mayst behold the Sun again.

From God's glances shrink thou never,
Meet them ever;
Who submits him to His grace,
Finds that earth no sunshine knoweth
Such as gloweth
O'er his pathway all his days.

Wakenest thou again to sorrow,
Oh! then borrow
Strength from Him, whose sun-like might
On the mountain-summit tarries,
And yet carries
To the vales their mirth and light.

Round the gifts He on thee showers,
Fiery towers
Will He set, be not afraid,
Thou shalt dwell 'mid angel legions,
In the regions
Satan's self dares not invade.

Von Canitz. 1654-1699.

IV.

Dayspring of Eternity!
  Dawn on us this morning-tide.
Light from Light's exhauſtleſs ſea,
  Now no more Thy radiance hide;
But diſpel with glorious might
          All our night.

Let the morning dew of love
  On our ſleeping conſcience rain;
Gentle comfort from above
  Flow through life's long parched plain;
Water daily us Thy flock
          From the rock.

Let the glow of love deſtroy
  Cold obedience faintly given;
Wake our hearts to ſtrength and joy
  With the fluſhing eaſtern heaven,
Let us truly riſe ere yet
          Life hath ſet.

Brighteſt Star of eaſtern ſkies,
  Let that final morn appear,
When our bodies too ſhall riſe
  Free from all that pain'd them here,
Strong their joyful courſe to run
          As the ſun.

To yon world be Thou our light,
  O Thou glorious Sun of grace;
Lead us through the tearful night,
  To yon fair and bleſſed place,
Where to joy that never dies
          We ſhall riſe.

Von Rosenroth. 1684.

V.

Once more from reſt I riſe again,
To greet a day of toil and pain,
    My Heaven-appointed lot;
Unknowing what new grief may be
With this new day in ſtore for me,
    But it ſhall harm me not
I know full well; my loving God
Will ſuffer not a hurtful load.

My burden every day is new,
But every day my God is true,
    And all my cares hath borne;
Ere eventide can no man know
What Day hath brought of joy or woe,
    And though it ſeem each morn
To ſome new path of ſuffering call,
With God I can ſurmount it all

Since this I know, oh wherefore ſink,
My faithleſs heart? And why doſt ſhrink

To take thy load again?
Bear what thou canſt, God bears thy lot,
The Lord of All, He ſtumbleth not;
Pure bleſſing ſhalt thou gain,
If thou with Him right onward go,
Nor fear to tread the path of woe.

My heart grows ſtrong, all fear muſt fly
Whene'er I feel Thy love, Moſt High,
Doth compaſs me around;
But would I have Thee for my ſhield,
No more to ſin my ſoul muſt yield,
But in Thy ways be found;
Thou God wilt never walk with me,
If I would turn aſide from Thee.

Dear God, let me Thy guidance find,
I follow with a contrite mind,
Oh make me true and pure;
As a good ſoldier I will fight
This world of ſin, and in Thy might
My victory is ſure;
Then bravely I can meet each day,
And fear it not, come what come may.

My God and Lord, I caſt on Thee
The load that weighs too ſore on me,
The yoke 'neath which I bow;
I lay my rank, my high command,
In my Almighty Father's hand,
Well knowing, Lord, that Thou
Wilt ne'er withdraw it, for Thy truth
Hath ever guided me from youth.

To Thee my kindred I commend,
For they are ſafe if Thou defend,
    Oh guard them round about;
My ſinful ſoul would ſhelter take
In Jeſu's boſom, for whoſe ſake
    Thou wilt not caſt her out;
When ſoul and body part at laſt,
Then all myſelf on Thee I caſt.

ANTON ULRICH,
Duke of Brunſwick. 1667.

EVENING HYMNS.

EVENING HYMNS.

I.

THE happy ſunſhine all is gone,
The gloomy night comes ſwiftly on;
But ſhine Thou ſtill, O Chriſt our Light,
Nor let us loſe ourſelves in night.

We thank Thee, Father, that this day
Thy angels watch'd around our way,
Warding off harm and vexing fear;
Through them Thy goodneſs guards us here.

Lord, have we anger'd Thee to-day,
Remember not our ſins, we pray,
But let Thy mercy o'er them ſweep,
And give us calm and reſtful ſleep.

Thy angels guard our ſleeping hours,
And keep afar all evil Powers;
And Thou all pain and miſchief ward
From ſoul and body, faithful Lord!

N. Hermann. 1560.

II.

Now reſt the woods again,
Man, cattle, town and plain,
The world all ſleeping lies.
But ſleep not yet, my ſoul,
For He who made this Whole,
Loves that thy prayers to Him ariſe.

O Sun, where is Thy glow?
Thou'rt fled before thy foe,
Thou yieldeſt to the night.
Farewell, a better Sun,
My Jeſus, hath begun
To fill my heart with joy and light.

The long bright day is paſt,
The golden ſtars at laſt
Beſtud the dark-blue heaven;
And like a ſtar ſhall I
For ever ſhine on high,
When my releaſe from earth is given.

My body haſtes to reſt,
My weary limbs undreſt,
I put away theſe ſigns
Of our mortality;
Once Chriſt ſhall give to me
That ſpotleſs robe that ever ſhines.

My head and hands and feet
Their reſt with gladneſs greet,
And know their work is o'er;
My heart, thou too ſhalt be
From ſinful works ſet free,
Nor pine in weary ſorrow more.

Ye limbs with toil oppreſs'd,
Go now and take your reſt,
For quiet ſleep ye crave.
Ere many a day is fled,
Ye'll find a narrower bed
And longer ſlumber in the grave.

My heavy eyes muſt cloſe,
Seal'd up in deep repoſe,
Where is my ſafety then?
Do Thou Thy mercy ſend,
My helpleſs hours defend,
Thou ſleepleſs Eye, that watcheſt over men.

Jeſus, my joy, now ſpread
Thy wings above my head,
To ſhield Thy little one.
Would Satan work me wrong,
Oh! be Thy angels' ſong,
"To him no evil ſhall be done."

My loved ones all, good night!
No grief or danger light
On your defenceleſs heads.
God ſend you happy ſleep,
And let His angels keep
Watch golden-arm'd around your beds!

Paul Gerhardt. 1653.

III.

THE day expires;
My ſoul deſires
And pants to ſee that day,
When whate'er hath vex'd her heart
Shall be done away.

The night is here,
Oh! be Thou near;
Chriſt, make it light within;
Drive away from out my heart
All the night of ſin.

The ſunbeams pale,
And flee and fail;
O uncreated Sun!
Let Thy light now ſhine on us,
Then our joy were won.

All things that move
Below, above,
Now with ſleep are bleſt;
Work Thou ſtill in me while I
Calmly in Thee reſt.

When ſhall the ſway
Of night and day,
Ceaſe to rule man thus?
When that brighteſt day of days
Once ſhall dawn on us.

Ah! never then
Her light again
Jerufalem fhall mifs,
For the Lamb fhall be her Light,
Filling her with blifs.

Oh were I there!
Where all the air
With lovely founds is ringing;
Where the faints Thee, Holy Lord,
Evermore are finging!

Lord Jefus, Thou
My reft art now,
Oh help me that I come,
Radiant with Thy light to fhine
In Thy glorious home!

FREYLINGHAUSEN. 1704.

IV.

THE moon hath rifen on high,
And in the clear dark fky
The golden ftars all brightly glow;
And black and hufh'd the woods,
While o'er the fields and floods
The white mifts hover to and fro.

How ftill the earth! how calm!
What dear and home-like charm

From ſilent twilight doth ſhe borrow!
Like to ſome quiet room,
Where wrapt in ſtill ſoft gloom,
We ſleep away the daylight's ſorrow.

Look up; the moon to-night
Shows us but half her light,
And yet we know her round and fair.
At other things how oft
We in our blindneſs ſcoff'd,
Becauſe we ſaw not what was there.

We haughty ſons of men
Have but a narrow ken,
We are but ſinners poor and weak.
Yet airy dreams we build,
And deem us wiſe and ſkill'd,
And come not nearer what we ſeek.

Thy mercy let us ſee,
Nor find in vanity
Our joy; nor truſt in what departs;
But true and ſimple grow,
And live to Thee below
With ſunny pure and childlike hearts.

Let death all gently come
At laſt to take us home,
And let us meet him fearleſsly;
And when theſe bonds are riven,
Oh take us to Thy heaven,
Our Lord and God, to dwell with Thee.

We sink to slumber now
Lord, in Thy name; do Thou
Forgive our sins, and o'er our heads
Keep watch the livelong night,
And let soft sleep alight
On us, and on all sick and painful beds.

CLAUDIUS. 1782.

FOR THE SICK AND DYING.

FOR THE SICK AND DYING.

I.

IN the midſt of life, behold
Death has girt us round.
Whom for help then ſhall we pray,
Where ſhall grace be found?
In Thee, O Lord, alone!
We rue the evil we have done,
That Thy wrath on us hath drawn.
Holy Lord and God!
Strong and Holy God!
Merciful and Holy Saviour!
Eternal God!
Sink us not beneath
Bitter pains of endleſs death,
Kyrie eleiſon.

In the midſt of death the jaws
Of hell againſt us gape.
Who from peril dire as this
Openeth us eſcape?
'Tis Thou, O Lord, alone!
Our bitter ſuffering and our ſin
Pity from Thy mercy win,
Holy Lord and God!
Strong and holy God!
Merciful and holy Saviour!

Eternal God!
Let us not despair
For the fire that burneth there,
Kyrie eleison!

In the midst of hell our sins
Drive us to despair;
Whither shall we flee from them?
Where is refuge, where?
In Thee, Lord Christ, alone!
For Thou hast shed Thy precious blood,
All our sins Thou makest good,
Holy Lord and God!
Strong and holy God!
Merciful and holy Saviour!
Eternal God!
Let us never fall
From the true faith's hope for all,
Kyrie eleison!

NOTKER tr. by LUTHER.
Written about 900, tr. 1524.

II.

GOD! whom I as love have known,
Thou hast sickness laid on me,
And these pains are sent of Thee,
Under which I burn and moan;
Let them burn away the sin,
That too oft hath check'd the love

Wherewith Thou my heart wouldſt move,
When Thy Spirit works within!

In my weakneſs be Thou Strong,
Be Thou ſweet when I am ſad,
Let me ſtill in Thee be glad,
Though my pains be keen and long.
All that plagues my body now,
All that waſteth me away,
Preſſing on me night and day,
Love hath ſent, for Love art Thou!

Suffering is the work now ſent,
Nothing can I do but lie
Suffering as the hours go by;
All my powers to this are bent.
Suffering is my gain; I bow
To my heavenly Father's will,
And receive it huſh'd and ſtill;
Suffering is my worſhip now.

God! I take it from Thy hand
As a ſign of love, I know
Thou wouldſt perfect me through woe,
Till I pure before Thee ſtand.
All refreſhment, all the food
Given me for the body's need,
Comes from Thee, who lov'ſt indeed,
Comes from Thee, for Thou art good.

Let my ſoul beneath her load
Faint not through the o'erwearied fleſh,

Let her hourly drink afresh
Love and peace from Thee, my God.
Let the body's pain and smart
Hinder not her flight to Thee,
Nor the calm Thou givest me;
Keep Thou up the sinking heart.

Grant me never to complain,
Make me to Thy will resign'd,
With a quiet, humble mind,
Cheerful on my bed of pain.
In the flesh who suffers thus,
Shall be purified from sin,
And the soul renew'd within;
Therefore pain is laid on us.

I commend to Thee my life,
And my body to the cross;
Never let me think it loss
That I thus am freed from strife—
Wholly Thine; my faith is sure
Whether life or death be mine,
I am safe if I am Thine;
For 'tis Love that makes me pure.

RICHTER. 1713.

III.

When the laſt agony draws nigh,
My ſpirit ſinks in bitter fear:
Courage! I conquer though I die,
For Chriſt with Death once wreſtled here.
Thy ſtrife, O Chriſt, with Death's dark power
Upholds me in this fearful hour.

In faith I hide myſelf in Thee,
I ſhall not periſh in the ſtrife;
I ſhare Thy war, Thy victory,
And Death is ſwallow'd up in Life.
Thy ſtrife, O Chriſt, with Death of yore
Hath conquer'd, and I fear no more.

Anon.

IV.

Lord Jeſus Chriſt, true Man and God,
Who boreſt anguiſh, ſcorn, the rod,
And diedſt at laſt upon the tree,
To bring Thy Father's grace to me;
I pray Thee through that bitter woe,
Let me, a ſinner, mercy know.

When comes the hour of failing breath,
And I muſt wreſtle, Lord, with death,
When from my ſight all fades away,
And when my tongue no more can ſay,
And when mine ears no more can hear,
And when my heart is rack'd with fear;

When all my mind is darken'd o'er,
And human help can do no more,
Then come, Lord Jeſus, come with ſpeed,
And help me in my hour of need,
Lead me from this dark vale beneath,
And ſhorten then the pangs of death.

All evil ſpirits drive away,
But let Thy Spirit with me ſtay
Until my ſoul the body leave;
Then in Thy hands my ſoul receive,
And let the earth my body keep,
Till the Laſt Day ſhall break its ſleep.

Joyful my reſurrection be,
Thou in the Judgment plead for me,
And hide my ſins, Lord, from Thy face,
And give me Life of Thy dear grace!
I truſt Thee utterly, my Lord,
For Thou haſt promiſed in Thy Word:

"In truth I tell you, who receives
My word, and keeps it, and believes,
Shall never fall God's wrath beneath,
Shall never taſte eternal death;

Though here on earth, in time, he die,
He is not therefore loſt; for I
Will come, and with a mighty hand
Will break away Death's ſtrongeſt band,
And lift him hence that he ſhall be
For ever in my realm with Me.
For ever living there in bliſs."
Ah let us not that glory miſs!

Dear Lord, forgive us all our guilt,
Help us to wait until Thou wilt
That we depart; and let our faith
Be brave and conquer e'en in death,
Firm reſting on Thy ſacred word,
Until we ſleep in Thee, our Lord.

PAUL EBER. 1557.

V.

Go and dig my grave to-day!
  Weary of my wanderings all,
Now from earth I paſs away,
  For the heavenly peace doth call;
Angel voices from above
Call me to their reſt and love.

Go and dig my grave to-day!
  Homeward doth my journey tend,
And I lay my ſtaff away
  Here where all things earthly end,
And I lay my weary head
In the only painleſs bed.

What is there I yet ſhould do,
  Lingering in this darkſome vale?
Proud, and mighty, fair to view,
  Are our ſchemes, and yet they fail,
Like the ſand before the wind,
That no power of man can bind.

Farewell earth then; I am glad
  That in peace I now depart,
For thy very joys are ſad,
  And thy hopes deceive the heart:
Fleeting is thy beauty's gleam,
Falſe and changing as a dream.

And to you a laſt good night,
  Sun and moon and ſtars ſo dear;
Farewell all your golden light;
  I am travelling far from here,
To the ſplendours of that day
  Where ye all muſt fade away.

Farewell, O ye much-loved friends!
  Grief hath ſmote you as a ſword,
But the Comforter deſcends
  Unto them who love the Lord.
Weep not o'er a paſſing ſhow,
To th' eternal world I go.

Weep not that I take my leave
  Of the world; that I exchange
Errors that too cloſely cleave,
  Shadows, empty ghoſts that range

Through this world of nought and night,
For a land of truth and light.

Weep not, deareſt to my heart,
 For I find my Saviour near,
And I know that I have part
 In the pains He ſuffer'd here,
When He ſhed His ſacred blood
For the whole world's higheſt good.

Weep not, my Redeemer lives;
 Heavenward ſpringing from the duſt,
Clear-eyed Hope her comfort gives;
 Faith, Heaven's champion, bids us truſt;
Love eternal whiſpers nigh,
"Child of God, fear not to die!"

E. M. Arndt.

VI.

Then I have conquer'd; then at laſt
 My courſe is run, good night!
I am well pleaſed that it is paſt;
 A thouſand times, good night!
But ye, dear friends, whom I muſt leave,
 Look not thus anxiouſly;
Why ſhould ye thus lament and grieve?
 It ſtandeth well with me.

Farewell, O anguiſh, pain, and fear,
  Farewell, farewell for ever!
It glads my heart to leave you here,
  Redeem'd from you for ever!
Henceforth a life of joy I ſhare,
  In my Creator's hand;
None of the griefs can touch me there,
  That haunt this lower land.

Who yet o'er earth in time muſt roam,
  Not yet from error free,
Scarce liſp the language of our home,
  The glad eternity.
Far better is a happy death,
  Than worldly life, I trow;
The weakneſs once I ſank beneath,
  I never more ſhall know.

Lay on my coffin many a wreath,
  For conquerors wreath'd are ſeen;
And lo! my ſoul attains through death
  The crown of evergreen,
That blooms in fadeleſs groves of heaven;
  And this fair victor's crown,
That mighty Son of God hath given,
  Who for my ſake came down.

'Twas but awhile that I was ſent
  To dwell among you here;
Now God reſumes what He hath lent,
  Oh grieve not o'er my bier;

But ſay, 'twas given at His command
Who takes it, He is juſt;
Our life and death are in His hand,
His ſervants can but truſt.

That ye ſhould ſee my grave, alas!
Shows we are frail indeed;
That it ſo ſoon ſhould come to paſs,
Our Father hath decreed;
And He your bitter grief ſhall ſtill.
Think not too young am I,
For he who dies as God doth will,
Is old enough to die.

Farewell, thou dear, dear ſoul, farewell!
To thoſe ſweet pleaſures go,
That we who mourning here muſt dwell,
Not yet, alas! can know.
Ah when ſhall that great day be come,
When theſe things fade away,
And thou ſhalt bid us welcome home;
Would God it were to-day!

Sacer. 1665.

VII.

My God, to Thee I now commend
My ſoul; for Thou, O Lord,
Doſt live and love me without end,
And wilt perform Thy word.

To whom elſe ſhould I make my plea,
That heavenly life be mine?
All ſouls, my God, belong to Thee,
My ſoul is alſo Thine.

Thou gav'ſt my ſpirit at my birth,
Take back what Thou haſt given;
And with the Lord I ſerved on earth,
Grant me to live in heaven.

My ſoul is ſprinkled o'er with blood
Thy Son hath ſhed for us,
And in Thy ſight is pure and good,
Adorn'd and radiant thus.

Thou my deliverer waſt of yore,
From ſin Thou mad'ſt me free,
Now, faithful God, doſt Thou once more
In death deliver me.

Thou liv'ſt and loveſt without end,
And doſt perform Thy word;
My paſſing ſoul I now commend
To Thee, my God and Lord!

HILLER. 1765.

FOR THE BURIAL OF THE DEAD.

FOR THE BURIAL OF THE DEAD.

I.

OH WEEP not, mourn not o'er this bier,
On ſuch death none ſhould look with fear;
He died as dies a Chriſtian man,
And with his death true life began.

Coffin and grave we deck with care,
His body reverently we bear,
It is not dead but reſts in God,
And ſoftly ſleeps beneath the ſod.

It ſeems as all were over now,—
The heavy limbs, the ſoulleſs brow,—
Yet through theſe rigid limbs once more
A nobler life, ere long, ſhall pour.

Theſe dead dry bones again ſhall feel
New warmth and vigour through them ſteal;
Reknit and living they ſhall ſoar
On high where Chriſt lives evermore.

This body, lying ſtiff and ſtark,
Shall riſe unharm'd from out the dark,
And ſwiftly mount up through the ſkies,
Even as the ſpirit heavenwards flies.

The buried grain of wheat muſt die,
Wither'd and worthleſs long muſt lie,
Yet ſprings to light all ſweet and fair,
And proper fruits ſhall richly bear:

Even ſo this body made of duſt,
To earth we once again entruſt,
And painleſs it ſhall ſlumber here,
Until the Laſt Great Day appear.

God breathed into this houſe of clay
The ſpirit that hath paſs'd away,
Chriſt gave the true courageous mind,
The noble heart, ye no more find.

Now earth has hid it from our eyes,
Till God ſhall bid it wake and riſe,
Who ne'er the creature will forget,
On whom His image He hath ſet.

Ah would that promiſed Day were here,
When Chriſt ſhall once again appear;
Then ſhall He call, nor one be loſt,
To endleſs life earth's buried hoſt.

N. Hermann. 1560.
After Prudentius.

II.

Now reſts her ſoul in Jeſu's arms,
  Her body in the grave ſleeps well,
His heart her death-chill'd heart re-warms,
  And reſt more deep than tongue can tell,—

Her few brief hours of conflict paſs'd,—
She finds with Chriſt, her Friend, at laſt;
She bathes in tranquil ſeas of peace,
  God wipes away her tears, ſhe feels
  New life that all her languor heals,
The glory of the Lamb ſhe ſees.

She hath eſcaped all danger now,
  Her pain and ſighing all are fled;
The crown of joy is on her brow,
  Eternal glories o'er her ſhed,
In golden robes, a queen, a bride,
She ſtandeth at her Sovereign's ſide,
She ſees His face unveil'd and bright;
  With joy and love He greets her ſoul,
  She feels herſelf made inly whole,
A leſſer light amid His light.

The child hath now its Father ſeen,
  And feels what kindling love may be,
And knoweth what thoſe words may mean,
  "Himſelf, the Father, loveth thee."
A ſhoreleſs ocean, an abyſs
Unfathom'd, fill'd with good and bliſs,
Now breaks on her enraptured ſight;
  She ſees God's face, ſhe learneth there
  What this ſhall be, to be His heir,
Joint-heir with Chriſt her Lord, in light.

The body reſts, its labours over,
  And ſleeps till Chriſt ſhall bid it wake;
The duſt that earth and darkneſs cover,
  Then as a ſun its tomb ſhall break.

Ah with what joy it rises then
To meet the perfect soul again!
Redeem'd from death, no more to sever,
 At that great marriage feast shall they
 With all the saints their homage pay,
And worship there the Lamb for ever.

We who yet wander through the waste,
 In faith long after thee on high;
While here the bread of tears we taste,
 We think upon that home of joy,
Where we (who knows how soon?) shall meet
With all the saints at Jesu's feet,
And dwell with Him for ever there.
 We shall see God; how deep the bliss
 We know not yet that lies in this;
Lord Jesus, come, our hearts prepare!

ALLENDORF. 1725.

III.

OH how blessed, faithful souls, are ye,
Who have passed through death; your God ye see;
 Escaped at last
From all the sorrows that yet hold us fast!

Here as in a prison we are bound,
Care and fear, and terrors hem us round,
 And all we know
It is but toil and grief of heart below.

While that ye are resting in your home,
Safe from pain, all misery o'ercome,
No grief or cross
Mixes with yonder joys to work you loss.

Christ doth wipe away your every tear,
Ye possess what we but long for here,
To you is sung
The song that ne'er through mortal ears hath rung.

Who is there that would not gladly die,
Changing earth for such a home on high,
Or who would stay
To toil amid these sorrows night and day?

Come, O Christ, release us from our post,
Lead us quickly hence to yonder host,
Whose battle won,
Now drink in joy and bliss from Thee our Sun.

SIMON DACH. 1650.

INDEX.

The numbers on the left hand are the numbers of the original hymns in the "Verſuch eines allgemeinen Geſang und Gebet Buchs," from which theſe hymns are tranſlated.

* No. 156 in the ſmaller collection.

* No. 73 in the ſmaller collection.

THE END.